Threats in the Age of Obama

MICHAEL TANJI (EDITOR)

DANIEL H. ABBOTT, CHRISTOPHER ALBON, MATT ARMSTRONG,
MATTHEW BURTON, MOLLY CERNICEK, CHRISTOPHER CORPORA, SHANE
DEICHMAN, ADAM ELKUS, MATT DEVOST, BOB GOURLEY,
ART HUTCHINSON, TOM KARAKO, CAROLYN LEDDY, SAMUEL LILES,
ADRIAN MARTIN, GUNNAR PETERSON, CHERYL ROFER, MARK
SAFRANSKI, STEVE SCHIPPERT, TIM STEVENS, SHLOK VAIDYA

NIMBLE BOOKS LLC

Nimble Books LLC

Nimble Books LLC

1521 Martha Avenue

Ann Arbor, MI 48103-5333

http://www.nimblebooks.com

The cover font, heading fonts and the body text inside the book are in Constantia, designed by John Hudson for Microsoft.

Contents

ABOUT THE AUTHORS

Daniel H. Abbott is a doctoral student at the University of Nebraska-Lincoln. He has previously written *Revolutionary Strategies in Early Christianity* and a chapter of *The John Boyd Roundtable*, both published by Nimble Books. He writes online at www.tdaxp.com.

Christopher Albon is a political science Ph.D. student at University of California, Davis. He researches the interrelationship between armed conflict and public health. Christopher writes about his research at WarAndHealth.com.

Matt Armstrong holds a Masters of Public Diplomacy and writes extensively on public diplomacy and strategic communication. Mr. Armstrong has presented at the U.S. Army War College, the National Defense University, Department of Homeland Security conferences, other Defense Department events, the Foreign Service Institute, and internationally. He is a member of the International Institute of Strategic Studies and The Public Diplomacy Council and blogs at (http://mountainrunner.us)

Matthew Burton was an intelligence analyst at the Defense Intelligence Agency from 2003-2005. After receiving a Master's degree from New York University's Interactive Telecommunications Program, he works as an online strategy consultant to the government and private organizations. An advocate for better Web-based collaboration and analysis tools, he and a group of partners recently created a virtual collaboration tool – Analysis of Competing Hypotheses – for the Intelligence Community's A-Space analytic environment. Matt frequently writes about the Internet's impact on government and democracy at personaldemocracy.com.

Molly Cernicek has worked and traveled extensively in the former Soviet Union, eastern and western Europe and has spent years watching Russia's science and technology sector transform from the

Soviet era leadership through the current evolution of the Russian government. She spent several years working at Los Alamos National Laboratory in the Department of Energy's Global Initiatives for Proliferation Prevention.

Dr. Christopher Corpora, President and CEO of Capitol Innovation and Strategy, is a regarded expert in nontraditional security threats who focuses on transnational organized crime and its role in the broader security environment. Dr. Corpora has a combined 17 years of military and civilian federal service. He earned his Ph.D. from American University's School of International Service and is currently an Adjunct Professor at both George Washington University and George Mason University's School of Public Policy.

Shane Deichman has spent nearly two decades in the national security field, as both a scientist and a manager. He led the Operations Division and the World Class Adversary Division at U.S. Joint Forces Command's J9 "Joint Futures Lab" for seven years, where concepts for future warfighting methods were challenged by adaptive adversaries. In 2008 he founded EMC2 LLC, a consulting company focused on emergency management and disaster preparedness. Shane blogs at Wizards of Oz, Dreaming 5GW, Antilibrary and ChicagoBoyz.

Matthew G. Devost is a technologist, entrepreneur, and international security expert specializing in counterterrorism, critical infrastructure protection, intelligence, risk management and cyber-security issues. Matt was co-founder of the Terrorism Research Center (TRC) in 1996 where he served as President and CEO until November 2008. Matt writes online at www.devost.net.

Adam Elkus is an analyst specializing in foreign policy and security. His work has been published in the Small Wars Journal, Athena Intelligence Journal, Defense and the National Interest, and the Huffington Post. He blogs at Rethinking Security, Dreaming 5GW, and the Anti-Library.

Bob Gourley, CDR USN (Retired) is a former U.S. naval intelligence officer. He is a career technologist whose last job in government was serving as the Chief Technology Officer for the Defense Intelligence Agency. Now a consultant, Bob shares his thoughts and ideas on technology and government at CTOVision.com.

Art Hutchinson is Founding Principal at Cartegic Group, a consultancy specializing in strategic thinking using interactive scenarios. He is a seasoned writer, speaker, advisor, and executive, having spent two decades working with management teams at some of the world's most prominent global organizations. Art writes extensively on the interplay between business strategy and rapid technology evolution and blogs at Mapping Strategy (cartegic.typepad.com/).

Tom Karako is the director of programs for the Claremont Institute, and the Salvatori Research Fellow in the American Founding. A doctoral candidate in political science at Claremont Graduate School, he has been an instructor for national security policy, American government, and constitutional law at Claremont McKenna College and California State University, San Bernardino. Tom is a member of the Independent Working Group on ballistic missile defense and the editor of Missilethreat.com.

Carolyn Leddy is an independent nonproliferation consultant. She formerly served as Director for Counterproliferation Strategy at the National Security Council. Ms. Leddy held a number of positions at the U.S. Department of State working on nonproliferation issues, and was an instrumental figure in overseeing the implementation of Libya's historic decision to give up its WMD programs. A former Professional Staff Member for the Committee on Foreign Relations in the U.S. Senate, she holds a B.A. from Sweet Briar College, and a Master of International Affairs from Columbia University.

Samuel Liles is an associate professor of computer information technology at Purdue University Calumet where he primarily researches offensive cyber warfare and the impacts on homeland security. Samuel came to Purdue Calumet from the telecom and information technology industry.

Adrian Martin is a crime analyst in Rochester, NY. He earned his Masters Degree in International Security from Georgetown and a degree in European History from Brown. He writes online at Politics & Soccer (a517dogg.blogspot.com).

Gunnar Peterson is a Managing Principal at Arctec Group. He is focused on distributed systems security for large mission critical financial, financial exchanges, healthcare, manufacturer, and insurance systems, as well as emerging start ups Mr. Peterson is an internationally recognized software security expert, frequently published, an Associate Editor for IEEE Security & Privacy Journal on Building Security In, an Associate Editor for Information Security Bulletin, a contributor to the SEI and DHS Build Security In portal on software security, and an in-demand speaker at security conferences. He blogs at (http://1raindrop.typepad.com)

Cheryl Rofer worked for the Los Alamos National Laboratory from 1965 through 2001 on topics including nuclear fuel cycle, fossil fuels, lasers, and environmental issues. She managed some of the Lab's environmental cleanups including those at a former Soviet uranium processing plant in Estonia and the assessment of radiological hazards at the former Soviet nuclear test site in Semipalatinsk, Kazakhstan. Cheryl writes online at Whirled View (whirledview.typepad.com/).

Mark Safranski is a teacher educational consultant and an adviser to a privately held Internet platform company, Conversationbase,

LLC. Mark blogs at Zenpundit, Chicago Boyz, Complex Terrain Laboratory and Progressive Historians.

Steve Schippert is a founder and member of the board of directors at the Center for Threat Awareness and Managing Editor of ThreatsWatch.org. A former United States Marine and veteran of the Gulf War, Steve's articles on the strategic and operational impact of national security decision-making have appeared in to the Weekly Standard and National Review.

Tim Stevens is a postgraduate student in War Studies at King's College London, researching information environments. He works at the International Centre for the Study of Radicalization & Political Violence. He also helps run the Insurgency Research Group at King's College London. Tim is also managing editor at the Complex Terrain Laboratory, and writes his own blog, Ubiwar.

Michael Tanji is a Senior Fellow at the Center for Threat Awareness and a Claremont Institute Lincoln Fellow. A former supervisory intelligence officer at the U.S. Defense Intelligence Agency, he spent two decades in strategic and tactical intelligence assignments in the Pacific Theater, the Balkans and the Middle East. Michael lectures on intelligence issues at George Washington University and writes online at Wired's Danger Room and ThreatsWatch.org.

Shlok Vaidya is the Energy Security Research Analyst at the Foundation for the Defense of Democracies' Center for Terrorism Research. He has written extensively about the impact of next generation warfare on energy infrastructure. Shlok is currently working on a book on the future of India's Naxalite insurgency.

ACKNOWLEDGEMENTS

As with any edited collection of work, none of this would have been possible without the generous support and hard work of the authors showcased herein. I was merely a temporary shepherd of their visions and thoughts and any disservice done to their labors is my fault entirely.

The seed of this particular effort was cast by Mark Safranski, editor of *The John Boyd Roundtable,* and Fred Zimmerman, Publisher of Nimble Books. It was Fred's idea that such a piece of work was necessary in the first place, and Mark - fresh off the success of his Roundtable effort - who unselfishly recommended me for the task.

Those most deserving of my thanks are my wife and children, whose patience and understanding granted me the time, space and energy necessary to bring this work to fruition.

THE THREAT LANDSCAPE

MICHAEL TANJI

Reasonable people can argue about whether or not our new President is taking office in a world that is any more or less dangerous than the one his predecessor has had to deal with for the last eight years. While the hot wars the U.S. and allied forces find themselves in the Middle East and Southwest Asia continue, we have a resurgent Russia and a rapidly emerging China threatening to bring about at least a temporary chill reminiscent of the last cold war. Few Presidents take office in the midst of a war, but unlike Truman—a combat veteran—President Obama assumes the mantle of Commander in Chief absent any practical military or national security experience at the strategic level, much less the operational or tactical.

While no one expects our nation's chief executive to be a master of all things—hence the existence of a cabinet—the fact that his key advisors and likely cabinet members are all veterans of a world that no longer exists (bi-polar, disconnected, industrial) suggest that the lenses through which they will view security affairs is likely to be out-of-focus. Today's primary problems are unconventional, networked, and global, and the shortcomings of industrial-age institutions and methodologies are increasingly obvious. The campaign mantra was "Change" but the formulation and execution of effective policy through "old hands" is most likely the first challenge our President will have to face.

This is not to say that outright or disastrous failure of the national security regime is inevitable, but we run the risk of slouching towards catastrophe if we continue to expect the world's most dangerous actors to behave in a fashion familiar to those who are about to assume positions of responsibility in the world's sole remaining superpower. What is sure to be a new situation for most of the old hands in this business is the granularity at which such strategic concepts will apply and the level of effort now required to deal with such threats at the sub- and extra-national level. How do you negotiate with an international assembly of non-state actors that convene, communicate and operate entirely in cyberspace? How do you deal with the actions of sub-national groups whose actions in seemingly local affairs in far-away places negatively impact daily life in the U.S. thanks to globalization? When is the last time anyone in a top national security job had to seriously entertain a discussion on what to do about pirates?

This is not a diatribe about real or perceived shortcomings of any individual or school of thought, but simply an attempt to plant the seed of an idea that we as a nation have little to lose by actually changing the way that we look at the problems we face. Such thinking is particularly important as astute observers will note that Russia and China are still national security problems; there is still no peace in the Middle East; and the various "wars" we have waged against drugs, poverty, terror, etc. have yet to see victory. It is not unreasonable to assume that we have reached a point at which old school approaches to any problem are not going to maintain the status quo: they are destined to set us back.

We approach these problems by looking at the most dynamic and confounding first. Issues related to non-state actors have long confounded even the most powerful states. In a networked world, where globalization works just as well for the black hats as it does for the white hats, such problems are achieving nearly insurmountable status.

No where is this point made clearer than in the world of international organized crime, where a dark nexus has formed where the world's worst people and the world's most dangerous materiel can reach down deep into the neighborhood level.

Yesterday it was narcotics, today it is counterfeit medication, next week its radiological material.

Consider the problem of terrorism. The "war on terror," while successful on many fronts, has still been a disproportionately expensive prospect that shows little sign of abating in the near future. We kill terrorists more or less at will, but there does not seem to be a shortage of new recruits. As our essay on terrorism explains, our ability to combat terrorism is flawed in some very fundamental ways.

The focus of threats today is increasingly pushed down to local levels. Size, however, masks the impact of these threats. Lightly armed pirates in motor launches impact global markets with their actions. The pointy-end of the world's most powerful militaries can be felled by microbes. The most important and influential aspect of a conflict may be driven motivations that do not fit neatly into the popular and widely accepted models, which begs the question: how effective will the problem solvers in an executive branch staffed with the "best educated" minds be if they are masters of all the wrong things?

As many false starts as we have had in the past with regards to the impact technology will have on our lives, it would appear that we are finally reaching the point where our ability to deal with any sufficiently serious issue—on any scale—is overcome by the pace and volume at which information flows. Old command-and-control models are not effective in a world where the virtual so rapidly and effectively impacts the corporeal. While it has long been the fashion to apply physical world metaphors to cyberspace issues (e.g. cyber deterrence, information warfare), the fact of the matter is that few in positions of responsibility truly have a grasp on the nature or impact of the information age. The most insignificant events from a technical or impact standpoint get the vast amount of our attention, serious problems that lack headline-grabbing glitz go unrecognized and under-appreciated, leaving us weaker and ever more vulnerable to attack. And while preventing attacks is probably the most important aspect of a national security capability, there is a very real possibility that we have reached a point where our inability to appreciate the operational environment leaves us in no better position today than we were in the winter of 1941.

Nuclear weapons and their proliferation is a long-standing problem that has yet to be adequately solved. In fact now, unlike any time in the past, the opportunity for nuclear holocaust is probably more significant than any time in the past, though not for obvious reasons. It was one thing for the two nations with the largest atomic arsenals to stand each other off, but as the number of nations (and possibly non-state actors) with real or suspected nuclear weaponry grows; the math gets much more complicated. Global thermonuclear war with just 30 minutes of warning is not the issue today; regional nuclear war or surprise attack most certainly is.

If you are on a mission to change the way government works, particularly in the national security arena, this is one of the few places where some independent and intellectually diverse thinking is to be found. It is with that in mind that we offer our view of some of the more pressing threats the Obama administration will have to deal with in these early days of the 21st century.

THE TANGLED RELATIONSHIP BETWEEN ORGANIZED CRIME, TERRORISM AND PROLIFERATION

CHRISTOPHER A. CORPORA, PH.D.

In a recent op-ed piece, Richard Clarke—the outspoken former U.S. White House Senior Advisor for Terrorism—suggested a complex possible scenario unfolding in the aftermath of the late-November 2008 Mumbai tragedies.[1] The scene Clarke sets demonstrates how inter-related terrorism, proliferation, organized crime and official corruption might combine to create a deeply negative situation for regional stability and global peace. The scene opens with a discussion between Taliban, new Pashtu anti-Karzai leaders, al Qaeda and Pakistani ISI about how these attacks were orchestrated to create a diversion in Pakistani efforts to better secure the FATA. In this story, the Mumbai atrocities were perpetuated to force more attention on Kashmir and make more space for the loosely linked partners to instigate a final dissolution of Pakistani sovereignty. If one teases out the logic of this scenario, it is easy to describe how drugs, arms and consumer goods trafficking provide the primary funds for the activities and the associated relationships through which these networks provide ease of clandestine movement and ability to target NATO and regional governments. The underlying theme is the need for a deeper strategic policy orientation—understanding how these seemingly separate activities and entities combine to present a potent threat to stability and eventual peace in the region. A full appreciation for this and similar, plausible scenarios requires a serious reconsideration of the traditional analytical separation between terrorism and crime, and its methodological exclusion from broader

---

[1] Richard A. Clarke, "What they're aiming at: the next chapter in the shadow war between the U.S. and al Qaeda," *Washington Post*, December 7, 2008 (B-1).

consideration as part of the on-going dynamic and complex political, economic, social and cultural environment in South Asia and the world.

The current global threat environment is complex and challenging—no longer bound by the realities and discourse of the Cold War. Despite the fact that the Cold War ended in 1991—with the fall of the Soviet Union—scholars and pundits continue to debate the new era and emerging paradigms for observing and acting in this environment. The classic Western approach towards understanding and explaining international security no longer fits within the theories and methods most reliably applied during the Cold War. The global security environment is no longer dominated by the U.S./Soviet conflict of words, policies and proxies. However, the analytical habits of the past have not given way to a comprehensible approach to current international security realities. The present threats to global security and stability increasingly come from non-state actors who are motivated to resist and undermine international conventions and sovereign rule to pursue bounded interests. Is it accurate or useful to analyze and assess these threats framed around the dominant resistant expressions—terrorists, traffickers, pirates and smugglers—or is there another way to understand and explain the activities associated with resistant non-state actors? What is the cost of continuing to assess these actors and activities in analytic "silos" of old security paradigms? How does this impact strategies and policies to address these nontraditional and often nonconventional threats? How would a multi-disciplinary set of theories and analytics assist in building a fuller understanding of these activities? These questions are best addressed by evaluating the changes in the nature and character of the security environment, questioning traditionally held a priori assumptions and constructing new models and metaphors to frame the current threat complex.

An occasionally intense debate exists in the global security dialog around proper ways to analyze and assess nontraditional, asymmetric threats to international peace and stability. This debate, a follow on from an earlier discussion about the proper objects of security studies, focuses on the proper ways to generalize about threatening activities, such as terrorism, proliferation and transnational crime.[2] Traditional approaches maintained separate conceptual spaces between these over-defined threats, sometimes relenting to the empirical evidence that these are not always divisible and distinct sets. However, the mainstream approach to these issues continues to be one that establishes separate industries around each activity. These are industries in that they cover a wide range of interlocutors from public, private and academic settings. Various experts and practitioners often focus on a single activity. This behavior is reinforced by the way the industry is networked— from specific governmental bureaucracies, through corresponding grants and funding programs, to narrowly focused studies, conferences and policies. These categories assume the state (or states) as the primary object of security studies—providing few conceptual tools to address non-state actors without treating them as mini-states. This over-specialization worked in the context of the Cold War—as most attention was placed on the activity in relationship to its role or place in the super power struggle. However, the end of the Cold War demonstrated how shallow this meta-narrative was in understanding global security—with little

---

[2] Louise I. Shelley is one serious scholar who has advanced several important thoughts about the convergence of international organized crime, terrorism and proliferation. See "Unraveling the new criminal nexus," Georgetown Journal of International Affairs, 6: 1 (Winter 2005) and "Methods and Motives: exploring links between transnational crime and international terrorism," (with John T. Picarelli, et al) NCJRS Document # 211207 (September 2005), www.ncjrs.gov/pdffiles1/nij/grants/211207.pdf. For an earlier, less conclusive consideration see "Methods not motives: implications of the convergence of international organized crime and terrorism," (with John T. Picarelli), Police Practice and Research, 3:4 (2002).

ability to anticipate its collapse and eventual outcomes of the period's end.[3]

These specific circumstances make it difficult to understand and analyze nontraditional threats as an inter-related set of social activities. The politics of security analysis favors specialization and separate treatment of a host of activities normally noted by the prefix counter. The tendency to study and comment on these activities as distinct forces dialog and inquiry to follow a similar path—so, the fields of counterterrorism, counter-proliferation, counternarcotics and counter-trafficking fall into separate governmental portfolios and corresponding academic and research buckets.[4] This is expedient from both a political and economic stand point, as separation allows for a broader array of intellectual turf emphasized by specialization, and economically following from government structures as one of the largest funding sources for the study of the various topics. A holistic, macro-level approach to these activities as part of a larger social construct does not conform well to the existing political and economic institutions that currently govern the field—despite empirical evidence to suggest otherwise.

The political and economic structure of the nontraditional threats field is further buttressed by three Cold War-era arguments.

---

[3] A slowly, growing group of scholars and experts increasingly recognize the anomalous nature of the Cold War. See K. M. Fierke, Barry Buzan and Steve Smith for several examples of this thinking. The re-emergence of English School Realism in the field of international security studies provides a wider window into the critique of neo-realism and neo-liberal institutionalism, which were the dominant theoretical security approaches during the Cold War.

[4] The proliferation of specialties is predicated by the way formal governing institutions approach these issues. Of course there is a symbiotic relationship between expert and governmental institutions. However, governments provide the largest pools of funding for research, so think tanks and academia tend to organize to these sources. One recent organizational development that may function as a change agent in this orientation is the establishment of the U.S. DoD's Office of the Deputy Assistant Security for Global Security Affairs – Counternarcotics, Counter-Proliferation and Global Threats.

First, terrorism, proliferation and global crime are best separated because they differ fundamentally in motivation and intent. Second, these are legally specific illicit, criminal conspiracies. Finally, the actors engaged in the activities are more often distinct than similar. Each of these arguments serves to support the reigning approach of separation and specialization and each suffers from deficiencies made clear by a review of the facts. This is not to say that differences do not exist. However, it is clear that closer attention to the similarities and relationship between these activities and actors can yield fresh ways to view and act in an environment that is increasingly frustrating for the traditional approaches. As the study of nontraditional threats becomes more sophisticated, and an object of an ever-growing reconsideration by many experts from disciplines not historically interested in these issues, new conceptual devices have helped address the complex nature and relationships found in this broader asymmetric complex.

Change

State conflicts fueled by ideological difference no longer dominate the security agenda. Conventional warfare is no longer the primary means to coerce a rival. States are not the only or most important actors in global conflicts. Yet, many analyses and corresponding policy actions continue to interpret the current global security environment through the lenses of state conflict and conventional force—lacking a focused attention on nontraditional actors, entities and techniques.[5] Many analysts and experts

---

[5] Historically, these issues are secondary issues in security studies, which focused on state actions and left these activities to criminology and legal studies. A review of the logic around the proliferation of new terminology that surfaced as these issues reemerged to broader analytic view in the early post-Cold War period suggests some of the struggle around transforming the way security analysts conceived the field. Operations other than war, special actions and an expanded sense of asymmetric threats were used to try to place the activities in the

continue to insist on treating nontraditional threats and irregular warfare as a separate and distinct activity—considered apart from state-centric, conventional conflicts—and where some try to account for the activities, they tend to use conventional methods as the basis of assessment.[6] This is especially true in the think-tanks and policy institutions found in the capitals of most developed states. These institutions are products of the Cold War and were established and tuned specifically to address the particular set of circumstances that dominated the strategic and security discourse over the last 50 years.

The initial post-Cold War security debate revolved around the proper objects of inquiry under the security rubric. Cold War-oriented strategic studies wanted to limit the range of acceptable items. However, others saw the empirical evidence for expanding the tent to allow for a more diverse set of activities. These debates were framed by Francis Fukuyama's declaration of history's end and Samuel Huntington's thesis on clashing civilizations. Each of these debates maintained a liberal democratic viewpoint that was most recently defined by a war of ideas—continuing to find similar conflicts in the rapidly transforming global security environment. After the September 11, 2001 tragedies, the discussion around what should be studied transitioned into a debate around how these issues should be analyzed. Currently, most experts and scholars agree that security studies has expanded, however, many continue to use Cold War conceptual artifacts, such as assumptions,

---

international security prism, but as the terms suggest the issues continued to be seen as outliers, peripheral to the core of the field.

[6] Even with the advent of promising sub-units, such as human factors, analyses continue to be driven by overly claustrophobic definitions and simplistic assessments of rationality with little attention paid to context and the inter-subjective, constructive nature of human behavior.

definitions, and categories based, in part, on factors that are no longer constant or relevant in the current context.[7]

Interestingly, the mid-1990s saw a slow, but meaningful shift in the way some security scholars observed and commented on global security. The rise in "new wars," regional and internal conflicts that favored nontraditional applications of force in support of a variety of issues that ranged beyond pure state interests (Kaldor, 2004). It became clear to this group of observers and experts that the end of the Cold War created a vacuum in large geographical and mental spaces for many around the globe. The ideological battle that served as a frame of reference for most contemporary international dialog was no longer relevant. Concurrent with this growing discussion and literature a louder "voice" was heard from the now fully dominant liberal democratic west. There were shouts of victory and heralding the end of history. Discussion quickly turned to the full internationalization of liberal democratic values and the corresponding liberal capitalist interpretation—giving rise to the notion of globalization, an epic change and direct descendent of most other major civilizational, political-economic paradigm shifts. The new debate and attempts to understand and explain the new security environment were framed by the way one understood the emergence or settling of globalization.

Several analysts and observers began to see the Cold War as a pause in a longer trend of nationalistic consolidation. These experts

---

[7] One of the clearest methodological challenges is the need to define an issue up front before studying it. This approach is particular to Western education, aimed at driving generalizations and methodological parsimony. However, the complex nature of these issues, constant change in variables and the increased volume and speed with which we receive data calls the accuracy of the approach into question. This is not to say that generalization is a poor method, but its results are limited by the stricture of building abstract frames separate from discovery and analysis. Wiki and blog technologies are popular examples of tools that can be used to develop knowledge interactively through construction, allowing flexible definitions to emerge and adhere to empirical data – if they are used properly.

argued that the dissolution of Yugoslavia and the Great Lakes region in Central Africa provided excellent evidence for understanding the Cold War as an historical anomaly. Yugoslavia, and much of the rest of Southeast Europe, once released from the constraints of the bi-polar halt, resumed its long historic exercise in defining its national identity. Gordon Bardos refers to this as a fourth wave of European nationalism, tracing the movement from 17th century consolidation of loosely aligned ethno-linguistic groups into a more homogenous narrative.[8] The growing assessment of African (and increasingly Asian) conflicts was similar in the assessment of the Cold War as an unusual pause in the historical trajectory of post-colonialism—the re-articulation of Africa on its own terms in the shadow of colonialism and the multiple surrogacy imposed on much of the continent by the superpowers in an effort to consolidate global support.[9]

These observations and analyses from the periphery of security studies loosely consolidated under an expanded security studies tent sometimes referred to as critical security studies.[10] This broader security focus is a collection of approaches represented by, but not limited to, human security (Ronnie Lipschutz and Caroline Thomas), diverse agency and interests (social construction dialog), securitization (Barry Buzan, Ole Waever and the Copenhagen School) transsovereignty (Maryann Cusimano-Love), world orders

---

[8] Gordon N. Bardos, "Prospects for stability in Southeastern Europe," *National Security and the Future*, 3:1-2 (2002). Bardos amplified his points in a roundtable discussion hosted by the journal in Zagreb, Croatia, August 2002.

[9] From this analytic view, one sees the post-colonial negotiation begin as it might have without the Cold War framing its context quickly after the development of the United Nations and its active mission to manage the colonial transition of power to self-governance.

[10] The term "critical security studies" was coined by Keith Krause and Michael Williams through a series of articles and workshops that concluded with an edited volume in 2000 and remains a useful collection of essays for understanding the argument for a change in the scope of the field. The concept of critical in the term is not limited to a New School Critical Theory approach, but based more on the use of the term by Robert C. Cox.

(Richard Falk), post-colonialism (Amartya Sen and Arjun Apparandai) and emancipation (Jurgen Habermas).[11] The underlying aim of the movement was to invite new voices and fresh perspectives into the security discussion—fomenting debate, collaboration and an intellectual architecture conducive to changing, challenging and enhancing the concept of security. Critical security approaches bring in new and historically silenced perspectives, adding the individual, non-state actors, normative concerns, and a re-characterization of political geography and economy outside of states. This change in the tone of security studies does not trivialize the state, but rather enriches the concept by putting it into analytical orbit with a variety of other legitimate social formations. It also provides an analytic venue to consider terrorism, proliferation and international crime as a proper object of security studies.

Challenging Assumptions

The concept of globalization establishes a useful structural metaphor to explore nontraditional threats as a part of a larger phenomenon that requires a different security optic. This idea frames speed, ease of access and rapid flows of knowledge, money and labor as critical structural variables, challenging linear conceptions of power and the core concepts of the state and sovereignty. Furthermore, and following from Michel Foucault, Paul Virilio and other similar-minded social theorists, these considerations suggest a much more universal understanding of power—not limited to physical coercive means and specific forms, but resident in any willful social actor or institution. The application of this frame to the current nontraditional threat

---

[11] The sourced individuals and debates are only meant to be exemplars and are by no means the only scholars or dialogs conducted in and around the various approaches. A broader genealogy of critical security studies can be found in K.M. Fierke's *Critical Approaches to International Security* (Cambridge: Polity Press, 2007).

environment provides a useful, empirical optic for evaluating the three arguments traditionally used to reinforce research differentiation and distinction.

Motivation

The artificial separation of the political from the economic establishes a conceptual foundation for making the claim for motivational difference between terrorism and organized crime. However, there is a political or ideological dimension to both terrorism and organized crime—just as there is an economic, social and cultural role for the activities and actors banded under the terms. The motivation for these actors and activities can only be fully understood within the context of the state and formal power— having a clear, causal relationship. This fact is seen readily in a short empirical survey of these actors across time and place. For example, the 19th century Sicilian Mafia and mid-20th century Colombian FARC were both founded on specific experiences of land reform in each place and time. They each took a different political economic outlook on these experiences—respectively and decidedly capitalistic and socialistic. Both entities were established in great part to address state weaknesses and a level of resistance to the intentions of formal power (Gambetta, 1999 and Castells, 2000). Arms trafficking has long been controlled and monitored by states as a direct or covert action mechanism to support a preferred party in a conflict. The "grey" arms traffickers tend to support specific political and economic ends. This is seen clearly in the sustained arming of Bosnian, Croatian and Albanian forces through the various protracted conflicts in 1990s Southeast Europe. Sanction breaking and evasion were almost always facilitated by a broad and interconnected network of international arms brokers with varying levels of informal support from a range of interested states and organized international ethnic networks. Interestingly, many of the elements that supported these entities against Serbian hegemony were at various (and sometimes simultaneously) times labeled as terrorists, criminals, freedom fighters and national heroes. Along these same lines, recent studies and investigative reports on Hezbollah, the Irish Republican Army, and the South Asian heroin trade suggest an ever more recognized relationship between political and economic motivations for these groups—making it increasingly difficult to distinguish between traditional differences in terrorist and organized crime activities.[12]

The logic of parsing motivation in traditional approaches to these issues cuts thinly along the assumption that terrorism is a political crime, as distinct from the economic crimes of organized crime and trafficking. This distinction made sense in a world where many conflicts were surrogates for a larger political ideological conflict. The term terrorism is a politically loaded concept, traditionally and currently used to distinguish between acceptable (or approved and funded) violent resistance to power and threats. As Ole Waver and others have suggested, defining a specific act or organization as terrorism allows the threatened party to classify the entity as a "security" issue that is illegitimate and illegal—pushing it into a separate category that is considered apart from other social behavior. The facts and acts of the entity have little to do with the actual pronouncement, which is predicated on acceptance. Making an act a "security" issue through the label of terrorism triggers a specific type of institutional action, corresponding with those and that deemed illegitimate. This is always done in a specific context from the reference point of a hegemonic entity—having the authority and coercive capability to make such distinctions.

---

[12] See Willem van Schendel and Itty Abraham, eds., *Illicit Flows and Criminal Things: States, Borders and the Other Side of Globalization,* Bloomington: University of Indiana Press, 2005; Peter Andreas, "Criminalizing consequences of sanctions: embargo busting and its legacy," *International Studies Quarterly,* 49, 2005; and Michael P. Arena, "Hizballah's global criminal operations," *Global Crime,* 7:3-4, 2006 for a short survey.

The case is similar for activities deemed as organized crime, where an activity falls outside of the surveillance and stated support of the state. In some cases the behavior is locally licit, acceptable and, in some cases, socially beneficial. It is perceived as an economic, moral and in some cases a political threat to established power structures because it circumvents formal authority. As Peter Andreas and Ethan Nadelmann suggest, the classification of activities and actors as criminal is an ever shifting line of legitimacy—beholden to a complex logic that flow through political, economic, social and moral/normative contexts.[13] This recognition is consistent with Oliver Wendell Holmes' pragmatic legal theory, positing the jurist as an interpreter of the times, in addition to being a scholar of the legal code.[14] Furthermore, Michel Foucault's diffuse conception of power provides an alternative logic for the understanding and explaining the history of illegitimacy by reintroducing the securitized activity and actor into the discussion. Foucault's sub-theme of parsed knowledge providing the conceptual foundations for over-valuing the role of formal power supports a need for a two-level methodology—considering the object/subject and its study—to objectively understand the full role of power in shaping the acceptable.[15] The historical, changing attitude toward slavery, piracy and substance prohibitions confirms the logic of these considerations and opens a window into a broader ability to survey complex relationships in the larger social space. However, the seclusion of the issue or entity enforces a set of assumptions and formal attitudes that limits the legitimate

---

[13] According to Andreas and Nadelmann in *Policing the Globe: Criminalization and Crime Control in International Relations,* (Oxford: Oxford University Press, 2006), historically, transnational crimes were categorized as political – the most threatening to a state or regime. The 18th and 19th century organization of professional and international policing activities (as distinct from military action) came from an increasing concern about political crime.

[14] Louis Menand, *The Metaphysical Club: A Story of Ideas in America,* (New York: Farrar, Straus and Giroux, 2001.

[15] James Faubion, issue editor, *Power: Essential Works of Foucault 1954-1984,* Paul Rabinow, Series Editor, Volume 3 (New York: New Press, 2000).

reconsideration of its status through a pejorative cloak that discourages consideration outside the bin of illegitimacy. In order to unlock this broader sense of power in the study of nontraditional threats, terrorism, proliferation and international crime need to be analyzed in their broader social context without the "scarlet letter" of illegitimacy—as a part of the empirical whole. This conceptual allowance allows the analyst and scholar to observe the relationship between these activities and others in a social context, providing new insight to the reasons and logic of the formation, role and operations.

Legal Interpretations

Following from the motivational dichotomy discussed above, traditional approaches interpret these activities as legally specific, illicit, criminal conspiracies – securitized and, as such, authorized for a level of scrutiny distinct and separate from legitimate social practices. The pronouncement of an organized criminal enterprise forces inquiry to be funneled through a specific legal lens – assuming the pejorative as fact. This act also presupposes a prosecutorial attitude, expecting a judicial act of some sort to render the activity inert – ranging beyond the conceptual isolation of the activities as threat, outside the realm of normal or acceptable social behavior. The corresponding jurisprudential logic drowns out other lines of inquiry, limiting the methods used to interpret the behavior.

This legal conditioning of the issues further highlights the limited debate in many developed nations around an acceptable renegotiation of the relationship between security and privacy. Defining terrorism, proliferation and international crime in largely legal terms pushes these issues outside into a distinct and limited analytical framework. Certainly, the legal optic is valid and useful, but the study of these issues is stifled by defining these social facts as ipso facto criminal. In taking an intellectual step back and observing these activities as part of a broader social context, new aspects, logics and trajectories become evident – spurring the possibility for different, creative and nuanced policies for action and engagement.

ACTIVITY DISTINCTION

The methodological tendency to define issues up front and build abstract frameworks for analysis leads to a cascading effect of micro-definition and differentiation – creating further subdivisions of specialization. The assumption that terrorists, proliferators and international criminals are more often distinct than similar is derived in no small part from these micro-specialties. The tendency to merge these definitions with action – countering – undermines the strategic goals and intent of fuller understanding and explanation in order to better inform regimes, laws and policy. The result is a methodological rush to a tactical approach and solution, based on incomplete analysis and unquestioned assumptions. This poorly conceived focus on what is commonly described as the "practical" pulls away from empirical relevance, often leading to policy failure and unintended consequences. Narrow definitions and theories analytically limit the range of full planning and the tactics, training and procedures necessary to amply execute and reach a well-articulated, desired effect.

A range of experts adhere to conceptual difference in defining terrorism, proliferation and international crime – focused on the specific activities or goals. Where the analytic stress is put on the differentiated activity, such as the smuggling of drugs being distinct from weapons or black-market compact discs, separate illicit methods and network suggests activities are analytically distinct. Another articulation of this position suggests that difference in the motivation behind the illicit behavior is the proper categorical variable – allowing for separate treatment of data based on the assessed character of motivating factors. Both of these approaches provide limited view into the larger nontraditional threat complex and limit important factors necessary for a strategic assessment of a given social context – illicit or otherwise. Categorization by activity assumes a low role for motivation and a dominant illicit behavior – the purpose of the activity is largely irrelevant and the entity is defined by its most obvious or recognized activity – essentially limiting the complex nature of the observed behavior in the wider social context, within and beyond the group or network. These approaches often do little to help navigate real-world situations, where illicit actors participate in a variety of social activities – legal and illegal. Also, the limited motivational consideration makes assessing the reasons for the activities secondary, inhibiting broader trend analyses and contextual considerations that could be useful in developing proactive policies and anticipatory enforcement strategies. This tendency to over-categorize often leads to a narrow understanding of the behavior and limits the ultimate range of influence by forcing the observer to develop policies in an artificially narrow analytical space.

THE (NOT SO) NEW THREAT COMPLEX

Increasingly, experts and scholars take a longer historical view, recognizing the Cold War as more of an anomaly than an enduring rule, and the tragedies of 9/11 and following events as a symptom of a lack of conceptual scaffolding. The aim of the analyses that come from this sensibility is to help explain the current dissonance between expectation and empirical facts in the broadest context possible. The larger intellectual space provided by critical security studies can help open new frontiers of possibility, but deeper change in strategic orientation is necessary to derive benefits from this approach. Several shifts in attitude and positive actions could help prepare the way and include the following suggestions for U.S. policy community:

Re-think the national security architecture to encompass these needs for new and enhanced understandings and approaches. Don't merely try to put a new faced on the National Security Act of 1947, but completely revitalize and renegotiate the posture and orientation—from strategy to organizational layout.

Create, participate in and support a broader educational environment—encouraging multi-disciplinary thinking and embracing the need to actively, re-conceptualize and intellectually retool for the current and future global security environment. As the past can often be a harbinger for the future, re-establish a national commitment to the Liberal Arts—as an institutional custodian of the history of ideas and critical thinking skills.

Consolidate national security expertise—practitioner and scholarly—de-emphasizing specialization and narrow categorization through a revamping of the planning and policymaking methods used to inform action.

Engage the world more honestly, building broader partnerships with shared leadership and focus on both similarities and differences across traditional boundaries—intellectual, cultural, economic and geo-political—recognizing the inter-related nature of each pursuit.

Specific suggestions as to how one might operationalize these strategic goals is best left to a robust dialog, founded on a common goal of reaching a set of over-arching, collaborative and integrated approaches to addressing these and future challenges.

The strategies and approaches needed to better understand and act in light of this nontraditional threat complex—the ever-changing, complex set of inter-related empirical realities and challenges that face global peace and stability—are not easy. Further complication comes with continued insistence on analytical over-simplification and generalizations that have little relevance in context. As Clarke clearly suggests, the world is a complex place where interests are wide and diffuse, coming together and separating in a non-particular way under a changing set of circumstances. The threat complex is not understood well using traditional assumptions, dichotomies and definitions. Professional analysts and scholars need to re-think the way they study and approach terrorism, proliferation and transnational organized crime to better inform the policy community. If the security analytic is not widened, more reflective and cognizant of empirical complexities and relationships then the international community runs an increasing risk of a continued and growing inability to fully see the bigger picture and its proper role in it.

THE TERRORISM MEME—LOOKING BEYOND THE CURRENT THREAT

MATTHEW G. DEVOST

In the past decade, the threat of terrorism has migrated from being a seemingly obscure and primarily academic threat concept to one of the principal influencers of our national security strategy. One of the primary appeals of terrorism is the ability to have a disproportionate impact with regards to the resources invested in the attack and the expected outcomes. To that extent, the terrorists have been extremely successful and will continue to be successful in the age of Obama.

True to its name, terrorism also seeks to strike terror into the hearts of its targets and influence behavior and outcomes through manifested fear and anxiety. This, fortunately, is a factor that requires internal reflection and can only be mitigated through a collective modification of existing societal perceptions in how we view and respond to the threat.

Terrorism has traditionally been an asymmetric problem. As such, it is becoming increasingly complex over time. Networks are more complex, the propagation of terrorism movements and ideals is facilitated through technology and global media, and the tools and tactics of terrorism are readily available to anyone with the resolve to perpetrate a conventional attack.

However, the purpose of this chapter is not to write about the terrorism we know, but rather the terrorism we can't quite see across the horizon. This chapter looks at terrorism not only as a present threat, but an emerging threat.

EMERGING THREAT ISSUES

Despite its historic implications over the past decade, it is important to still view terrorism as an emerging threat issue. This is important for several reasons:

The depth and scope of global terrorism movements appears to be increasing due to the proliferation of technology accelerated self-organizing cells.

Terrorist organizations will continue to realize their objective of disproportionate impacts against targeted societies. This makes terrorism an attractive tactic over the near to mid-term.

Terrorist organizations will be able to augment the impact of their attacks through technological exploitation taking advantage of the expected future proliferation of weapons of mass destruction.[16]

Our efforts to combat terrorism, while effective in some regard, will never be absolute and modern societies will remain in a perpetual state of vulnerability. Until we learn to manage that vulnerability in the context of total risk, terrorists will continue to realize disproportionate psychological impacts as well.

Global terrorism groups have begun migrating from centralized and modestly structured organizations to global movements. This, if it hasn't already, will soon become a persistent meme unto itself. To that extent, "terrorism" is perhaps the most effective negative global meme of the past decade. This migration from group to movement to meme is increasingly concerning.

---

[16] For additional dialogue on the issue of WMD terrorism see: *World At Risk: The Report of the Commission on the Prevention of WMD Proliferation and Terrorism.* Available for free online at: http://www.preventwmd.org/report/. Additionally, see the book by Brian Jenkins: *Will Terrorists Go Nuclear?* (Amherst, New York: Prometheus Books, 2008).

Most significantly, in the next 5-10 years we will start to see an alignment of capability and intent.

To date, terrorist attacks, with some "Black Swan" exceptions[17], have operated within a restricted capability environment. As capability and intent become aligned due to technological proliferation, the potential impact of global terrorism significantly increases.

To understand what the future might hold, a more in-depth look at these issues is required.

SELF-ORGANIZING CELLS

Is terrorism an anthill or the Howard Dean Presidential campaign? Probably both.

Regardless of the exact model, it is clear that terrorist groups have taken on emergent properties facilitated initially by the global movement that is the modern day al Qaeda and migrating towards emergent properties associated with terrorism as a meme. One need only look at the structure of the terrorist cells that attacked targets in London and Madrid to recognize their emergent properties. Both cells were composed of like-minded individuals organizing, planning, and executing attacks with no strong links to the al Qaeda group, but rather with an affinity for the al Qaeda movement.

These self-organizing cells may be less dangerous (overall) in the near-term, however, they are increasingly difficult to detect and counter, especially at the national strategic intelligence level. These self-organizing cells bring additional credence to the notion that

---

[17] For an enlightening and thoughtful analysis of the Black Swan concept, see: Nassim Nicholas Taleb, *The Black Swan: The Impact of the Highly Improbable* (New York: Random House, 2007).

"all terrorism is local" and the requirement for focused local intelligence capabilities.[18]

It might be useful to classify future terrorist cells into three distinct categories:

Core cells have strong ties and support from the centralized terrorist organization. The attacks of September 11 would be easily categorized as a core cell given their direct exposure, communication, training, and receipt of resources from the formal al Qaeda organization.

Franchise cells have no strong ties to the formal terrorist organization, but may have some enabling communication or "license to operate" from the core. This enabling connection also seeks to motivate and instigate the cells potential for action. Perhaps the best analogy for this type of influence is a blend of "starstruck" and "peer pressure." If those that shook Sinatra's hand are more prone to adhere to the unwritten rules of Las Vegas, those that receive support from bin Laden are more likely to manifest their attack.

Emergent cells have no formal ties to the core, but rather show an affinity for the movement or a susceptibility to the terrorism meme. Increasingly in these instances, technology will emerge as an enabler to the cell providing them a way to communicate, radicalize, plan, and train/develop materials for the attack.

In the opening sentence of this section, I referenced the Howard Dean[19] campaign as an analogy for a terrorist movement.[20] Let's take a few paragraphs to put that statement in context.

---

[18] In matters of local intelligence analysis, I will admit to being extremely biased towards the model propagated by John Sullivan and the Los Angeles Terrorism Early Warning Group.

Governor Dean's 2004 presidential campaign was ground-breaking in several regards, but most interestingly for our analysis is that it serves as a great model for a self-organizing movement (with its own associated self-organizing campaign cells) and in my analysis, the early propagation of a meme, which we'll simply call "change."[21]

Governor Dean's campaign was unique in two important areas. First, it leveraged technology to increase the efficiency and scope of the campaign in ways that hadn't been done before using new tools that didn't exist in prior campaigns. Simply put, he took advantage of the tools available to him to campaign in non-traditional ways to create a mild form of "technology surprise". Secondly, he decentralized the campaign structure to enable the growth of a movement, via what is often referred to as "grass roots" participation in unique unstructured ways.

This decentralization motivated supporters to campaign in innovative ways and allowed for later acknowledgement by the formal campaign if they liked what these self-organizing groups were doing. This is quite similar to what we've seen with the London and Madrid attacks with al Qaeda leadership acknowledging and supporting the attacks after they "liked what they saw." A simple timeline would note: movement inspires group to action, group takes action, movement absorbs group post-action, and the overall movement is strengthened.

---

[19] By no means do I seek to associate fellow Vermonter and hockey player Howard Dean with the global al Qaeda terrorism movement. This analogy is meant to provide academic context to the concept of emergent groups, not suggest any connection or correlation between Governor Dean and terrorism as none exists.

[20] I would be remiss to not include a citation to Eric Hoffer's *The True Believer: Thoughts on the Nature of Mass Movements*, most recently reprinted through Harper Perennial Modern Classics (New York: 2002).

[21] I am intentionally simplifying what is a rather complex dynamic to illustrate a point. Political scientists please take a deep breath and roll with it. There is more over simplification to come.

In many ways, Governor Dean set the stage for the emergence of Senator Obama by demonstrating an effective roadmap for technology utilization, grassroots campaigning, and setting the seeds for the propagation of the "change" meme.

In the United States, the negative enablers[22] of the "change" meme appeared to be dissatisfaction, discontent, lack of opportunity, and so on. Of course, the underlying action for the "change" meme is democracy, campaigns, and the electoral process. If we look closely at the "terrorism" meme, we might see some of the same negative enablers, but unfortunately, the underlying action is the act of terrorism itself. To address the problem of terrorism, we must look at it not only from the perspective of eliminating those radical elements that seek to perpetrate crimes against humanity, but must also look at the positive and negative enablers of the emerging terrorism meme.

In the example above we discussed Governor Dean as the early manifestation for the "change" meme and the role-model for technology adoption and campaign strategy in the Obama campaign. In that sense, one might look at al Qaeda as the early manifestation of something bigger. The question is....what?

MegaTerrorism

It is probably realistic to assume that any terrorism movement is not sustainable over the very long-term without some sort graduation to something bigger and/or different. In earlier movements the natural migration was that of eradication or disbandment for lack of resources or the migration to a legitimate political entity. In the context of a group like al Qaeda, their propensity to engage in large scale attacks that garner the global condemnation of the existing political systems makes it is hard to

---

[22] The use of the term negative enablers is meant to convey those negative factors that positively impact the propagation or adoption of the meme.

imagine their migration in the current context to anything that will be acceptably legitimate. What we should seek to prevent is a scenario where al Qaeda emerges as unacceptably legitimate.

One cannot accurately predict what a future al Qaeda looks like, but we can predict what we don't want it to look like. Here are two scenarios we should be looking to prevent:

al Qaeda emerges as a mega-terrorism movement based on a widespread global affinity for the "terrorism" meme. Self-emergent and franchise cells become the "global guerillas"[23] of modern society and disruption of social integrity leads to a diminished quality of life for all.

al Qaeda shoehorns its way to legitimacy through the proliferation of technology that enable it to develop a sustainable WMD program. The most frightening scenario is not a terrorist organization with one nuclear weapon, but with two.[24] One to use or demonstrate possession (let it be found on the streets of NY) and one to threaten future attacks. The barrier to other WMD from a technological perspective almost assumes the ability for repeat attacks.

An essential element of counterterrorism strategy is to look at what we hope to prevent and preventing both of the above scenarios would seem to be legitimate long-term goals. From a more near-term perspective, we should plan for innovative use of societal infrastructures as weapons by terrorists against us and the continuance of brute-force terrorism.

"KILL WITH A BORROWED SWORD" AND URBAN TAKEDOWNS

---

[23] If you are reading this chapter, you owe it to yourself to spend some time at John Robb's Global Guerillas blog: http://globalguerrillas.typepad.com/globalguerrillas/
[24] I am paraphrasing a scenario shared with me by friends Sebastian Junger and Walter Purdy based on interviews they conducted in the Tri-border region and dinner discussions with terrorism expert Brian Jenkins.

When looking at the threat of terrorism in the near-term, there are two clear attack trends. The first involves the use of infrastructures in innovative and unexpected ways. The second relies on the inevitable availability of small arms, explosives, and soft targets.

"Kill with a borrowed sword" is an ancient Chinese stratagem that dictates using the capabilities of the adversary against them. We have seen the modern day equivalent of "kill with a borrowed sword" with the attacks of September 11. A terrorist organization like al Qaeda does not have the capability to build missiles that can be delivered with the level of explosive and incendiary impact and the level of precision that was directed against the World Trade Centers on that day. al Qaeda was, however, able to successfully weaponize an infrastructure with great impact. In counterterrorism circles this type of attack has been described as low-tech/high-concept and we should continue to look at ways future infrastructure weaponization can be prevented.

The other near-term scenario for attacks is what might be described brute-force attacks or as articulated by John Robb as "Urban Takedowns"[25]. A perfect example of this scenario was presented by the attacks in Mumbai, India. According to early reports, the terrorists used automatic weapons, simple explosives, commercially available communications devices (cell phones) coupled with the element of surprise against soft targets to inflict hundreds of casualties. Unfortunately, for as long as there are perpetrators willing to engage in this style of terrorism, open and free societies will be infinitely vulnerable to attack. Accounting for this threat in the context of risk management will be an essential element of future counterterrorism strategies, but we will never be risk free.

---

[25] http://globalguerrillas.typepad.com/globalguerrillas/

Displaced Terrorists

The emergence of global terrorist movements like al Qaeda also creates an environment of displacement for other more traditional terrorist organizations that sought to use terrorism as tactic of calculated political violence.

How does displacement work? As an example, let's look at hijacking as a terrorism platform. Prior to September 11, there were over 1000 hijackings of aircraft, yet only one with known intention of using the plane as a weapon of mass destruction.[26] Hijacking fell into three general categories:

- Geographic escape. To move from country A to country B.
- To attract attention to a particular group or cause.
- To use the plane and/or passengers in political negotiations.

Discounting category one, what is a terrorist organization that formerly utilized hijacking as a calculated political tool to do? Any attempt to hijack an aircraft in a post September 11 environment will be viewed as a potential attempt to use the plane as a WMD and the perceptions and procedures that were effectively (though briefly[27]) exploited on September 11 are no longer in play. Moreover, the use of hijacking now suffers from the "top this" syndrome: merely hijacking a plane, without using it as a WMD, now appears rather unimpressive. Hijacking has been displaced as an effective political tool.

---

[26] Experts cannot agree on the exact number, but most agree it is 1000+. With regards to using the plane as weapon of mass destruction, review the details associated with the December 24, 1994 hijacking of Air France Flight 8969.
[27] One could argue that the use of technology allowed for the rapid adaptation of perceptions based upon real-time information garnered from cell phones and air phones regarding the terrorists' intent to use the plane as a WMD by the passengers of United Airlines Flight 93.

This displacement represents not only a legitimate future threat, but also an opportunity to reduce the appeal of the overall terrorism meme by attempting to divert or funnel displaced groups towards alternative means of political negotiation that do not involve violence. If not, it is highly likely the displaced groups will adopt new tactics and strategies to compensate for their displacement or will escalate their activities to obtain appropriate "market share" in a world where the costs inflicted by terrorism are steadily increasing.

CYBERTERRORISTS

One of the most widely discussed, but least realized future tactics is the use of cyberattack against critical infrastructure. Cyberterrorism is likely to be attractive, particularly for displaced and conventional terrorists for the following reasons:

Attacks impacts are disproportionate to the resources required to execute the attack. Once appropriate knowledge is obtained, cyberterrorism can be perpetrated with very few resources.

Attackers do not need to be geographically located with the attacker. With conventional terrorism the attacker must obtain geographic proximity to the target. With cyberterrorism, the nature of global networks enables an attacker to be geographically isolated from the target.

Cyberattacks can be continually perpetrated with existing resources. A suicide bomber is good for one attack. A cyberattacker can be used repeatedly and the current state of attribution indicates a smart attacker could operate indefinitely.

Cyberattacks can be used to augment or increase the impact of traditional attacks.

While difficult to perpetrate, cyberattacks could be used to disrupt the physical operation of critical infrastructures that results in the loss of life or physical harm and damage. From a terrorist perspective, this is a best-of-both-worlds scenario that becomes highly attractive.

Critical infrastructures are vulnerable to cyberattack, providing the same universal appeal as soft targets using brute force methods.

Cyberattacks attract tremendous media attention and could serve as a viable substitute for those groups that used hijackings to attract attention to a particular group or cause. They might also be used as a platform for political negotiation.

Using cyberattack to have a sustained impact on a critical infrastructure is not necessarily an easy objective, but it is one that will be actively pursued by terrorist organizations in the near to mid-term. In fact, experts are increasingly curious as to why it hasn't happened yet.[28]

CONVERGENCE

Increased cooperation between terrorist organizations, organized crime, rogue states, and other international entities will introduce new dynamics to the current threat environment. Globalization is not just a nation-state initiative, it is occurring within threat groups as well.

Failed states and ungoverned geographic regions will continue to serve as nesting grounds for this global underbelly of asymmetrical threats and their increasing cooperation will allow for the cross-fertilization of capabilities and the bartering of resources.

Addressing failed and forgotten states will be critical in diminishing the future threat of terrorism.

CONCLUSION

---

[28] Including the author himself.

The prevailing wisdom dictates that terrorism is something that we defeat or something we can declare war against. Proposing that we can "win" against modern terrorism is like proposing that we can "win" at chess under the following obscene circumstances:

We have conditioned ourselves to only look at the board one move at a time.

Our adversary gets to introduce new pieces randomly every time one is lost.

We aren't capable of seeing all of the adversary's pieces.

The chessboard is a puzzle that has only been partially completed.

While we can defeat particular adversaries and should continue to do so, solving the problem of terrorism as a meme will require a more sophisticated long-term approach. We should seek to establish foreign policy and programs that diminish the attractiveness of the emerging terrorism meme and seek to understand why in some circumstances it is as attractive to some as a new pair of Nike shoes is to others.

To follow the chess analogy above, we must:

- Develop an ability to look several moves into the future and attempt to better understand the consequence of each action. In addition, learn to see ourselves from the adversary's perspective.

- Improve our ability to identify and dismantle adversary resources to include personnel and support. This will require precise and focused initiatives to dismantle structured terrorist organizations.

- Universally improve our intelligence capabilities.

- Deconstruct the terrorism meme and establish strategies to prevent it from spreading and adapting in undesirable ways.

The first three bullets seem reasonably achievable, but without addressing the fourth we have no long-term strategy to combat terrorism.

Lastly, to reduce the impact of global terrorism, we need to modify our perceptions as a society and look at terrorism in the context of total risk while adopting a risk management approach. To expect that we can be protected from all terrorist attacks is unrealistic and we must learn to accept and manage terrorism like any other risk. The disproportionate impact of conventional terrorism has been coupled with disproportionate responses which are not sustainable in the long-term.

We cannot eliminate all vulnerabilities and the cost of eliminating some may be too high, not only from a resource perspective, but in keeping with the principles that make our nation great.

We cannot eliminate all terrorism threats, but we can seek to diminish the environment in which threats manifest themselves, whether that be in the context of "hearts and minds", eliminating physical sanctuaries, or improving the conditional environment that allows the terrorism meme to propagate.

Until we start looking at terrorism not only as an act that can be perpetrated, but a meme that can dangerously propagated, we will face an increasingly uphill battle.

CRAZY AS A FOX

ADRIAN MARTIN

Do "normal" people blow themselves up to send political messages? Do "normal" people drop out of school to sell drugs on a street corner? Blowing yourself up in a suicide bomb seems irrational to most observers. Some analysts even chalk actions like these up to pure rage and anger. Similarly, many people dismiss gang members as irrational and stupid, because why else would someone throw away their future to end up in jail? But to accept explanations like these does harm by throwing away an opportunity to study what is really going on. Rather than attempting to replace one ideology (jihadist Islam, thug culture) with another (democracy, mainstream American culture), economic analysis looks at why and under what circumstances individuals make the decisions they do. Using this tool, we can even see why a rational individual would blow themselves up or would drop out of school to sell drugs.

The basic assumption of traditional economic analysis (also known as rational choice analysis) is that individuals make decisions rationally under constraints and incentives. Rational behavior really just means that whatever pre-existing goal an individual has, they choose the best identifiable means to achieve it. Goals are not held to a standard of rationality but instead are taken as a given. An individual's goals generally tend to be the maximization of some ideal combination of goods, whether those goods are easily measurable like money or rank, or social, like prestige, affection and companionship.

Although economic analyses share the same fundamental assumptions and outlook, different economic analyses can still reach opposite conclusions. It's important to use knowledge of micro-conditions so that any analysis is correctly informed as to goals and incentives. One of the models of this type of analysis is Stathis Kalyvas's work on creating a model of civilian behavior in civil war, which was based on intensive study of the Greek civil war in the 1940s. [29] Kalyvas looks at the constraints imposed on civilians in civil war, the incentives given to them, and how the phenomenon of denunciations and defections create institutions that shape civilian decision making.

As mentioned above, economic analysis can arrive at different conclusions based on the goals assumed to each decision-maker. In terms of organizations, there are two traditional theories. One theory, the classical model,[30] states that organizations simply attempt to achieve their stated goals. For example, al Qaeda attempts to create a global caliphate. This is the approach used by Ronald Wintrobe to show the train of logic that can lead a rational organization to use terrorism, even suicide terrorism.[31] Wintrobe assumes that the leaders of an organization with extreme political goals will take actions to further those goals, regardless of the cost to the organization (for instance, disbandment if the organization's goals are achieved). Wintrobe concludes that organizations with extreme goals and little ability to compromise will have a demand for extreme methods, such as terrorism.

The other theory states that organizations attempt to survive even at the expense of their stated goals—that social incentive for solidarity and the camaraderie associated with the organization is more important than the organization's goals. This theory would argue that an organization such as a youth gang engages in criminal

---

[29] Stathis Kalyvas. The Logic of Violence in Civil War . Cambridge University Press, New York, 2006.
[30] "Classical model" versus "natural systems model" terminology taken from Max Abrahms, "What Terrorists Really Want." International Security, 32:4, pages 78-105.
[31] Ronald Wintrobe. "Extremism, Suicide Terror, and Authoritarianism." *Public Choice*, 2006, 128:169-195.

activity in order for the individuals involved to maximize the friendship and solidarity it generates rather than the material benefits of their activity (thus they would still join gangs even if more legitimate economic opportunities existed). A good example is Larry Iannaccone's work looking at religion from a rational actor perspective. Religious sects are built to solve the problem of "free riders," defined as members of the organization who contribute nothing to the organization, but consume the organization's goods. Kicking members out who do not adhere to certain norms of behavior leads to intense solidarity amongst the members and an efficient goods and service delivering organization.[32]

In the interest of illustration, this chapter will explore both models, beginning with the first, as we examine how al Qaeda in Iraq attempted to achieve its goals, and in so doing was rationally led to use extreme terrorism.

In Iraq, America's goal was "an Iraq that is peaceful, united, stable, democratic, and secure."[33] Essential to the achievement of American goals in Iraq was the maintenance of an Iraqi national identity that included both Sunni and Shia Arab communities. This goal was in direct opposition to the goals of al Qaeda in Iraq (henceforth just al Qaeda or AQIZ), which sought a Sunni Islamic Caliphate that would rule the nation. That goal required the destruction of the Iraqi nationalist identity and its replacement with a (Sunni) Islamic identity. We will take the goal of al Qaeda, that of an Islamic Caliphate to replace states in the Middle East and therefore the creation of an Islamic identity, as a given, and assume that al Qaeda rationally attempted to achieve this goal.

To achieve its goal of eliminating the Iraqi nationalist identity which included Sunnis and Shias, AQIZ needed to create a self-

---

[32] Larry Iannaccone and Eli Berman. "Religious Extremism: The Good, the Bad and the Deadly." *Public Choice, 206, 128:109-129.*
[33] National Strategy for Victory in Iraq. White House.

sustaining cycle of violence between Sunni and Shia communities, and needed to eliminate the state's monopoly on legitimate violence and provision of social services. AQIZ attempted to accomplish the first objective in three ways. First, they launched information campaigns portraying local personal violence in political terms.[34] Second, they attacked "linking nodes" between Sunni and Shia communities, such as mixed marriages and mixed neighborhoods.[35] Increasing the social distance between Sunni and Shia increased the cost to an individual to overcome AQIZ propaganda.[36] Third, they attacked social *schwerpunkts*[37] —targets that have the ability to cause cascading social collapse (for example, important religious shrines).[38] To eliminate the state's monopoly on violence and social services, al Qaeda had to perpetuate regular acts of violence and target the state's social services, making it too dangerous for state employees to go to work. The goal of these tactics was to create a market environment for security and social services, in which the population of Iraq would be forced to search for outside providers of these services. [39] These providers were either tribal, neighborhood-based, or sectarian militias (or some combination of the three). As Iraqis received security and social

---

[34] Kalyvas shows how many instances of personal violence are reinterpreted through political lenses in civil wars in both The Logic of Violence in Civil War as well as a shorter article: Stathis Kalyvas. " The Ontology of " Political Violence" : Action and Identity in Civil Wars." *Perspectives in Politics* , Vol 1, No 3, Sept 2003, pgs 475-494.

[35] Sudarsan Raghavan. " Marriages Between Sects Come Under Sige in Iraq." *Washington Post* . March 4, 2007. Page A16. Online at http://www.washingtonpost.com/wp-dyn/content/article/2007/03/03/AR2007030300647.html.

[36] Glaeser, Political Economy of Hatred.

[37] A *schwerpunkt*, a term from German blitzkrieg warfare, refers to the focal point of an attack, and where the blitzkrieg forces hoped to break through enemy lines.

[38] John Robb. *Brave New War: The Next Stage of Terrorism and the End of Globalization* . John Wiley & Sons, Hoboken NJ, 2007. Pg 96.

[39] For instance, from a letter by Zarqawi in February 2004 provided by the United States: "If we succeed in dragging them [the Shia] into the arena of sectarian war, it will become possible to awaken the inattentive Sunnis as they feel imminent danger and annihilating death at the hands of these Sabeans." Available on the US Department of State website, http://www.state.gov/p/nea/rls/31694.htm.

services from these non-state groups, their identities devolved away from nationalism and towards either tribal or sectarian identities.

Iraqis fell back to tribal security forces where possible instead of sectarian militias due to lower entry costs. Many Iraqis already had tribal identities, however they were not initially part of sectarian militias. Obtaining protection and social services from an organization that you already at least partially identify with means you pay the lowest "cost" for the desired return. Thus in areas where tribes are strong, such as Anbar province, tribal security forces replaced the state, because of zero start-up costs for the tribes and low entry costs for affiliated individuals. In areas where tribes have been crushed or are weak for other reasons like a high population of migrants with fewer roots to their communities,[40] Iraqis might fall back to sectarian militias for security instead. In areas where sectarian groups and tribes are in opposition, sectarian groups will have a key advantage—because sectarian membership is more voluntary than tribal membership, sectarian militias will not be forced to extend benefits based on kinship, thus mitigating a free rider problem of tribes. Instead, recipients of protection and services form a neighborhood militia.

From al Qaeda's point of view, it would have been preferable that the population fall back on sectarian militias. Tribes provide an alternative political organization to the Caliphate, and also cut across sectarian identities, with many tribes incorporating both Sunni and Shia branches. Tribal conflict would have reframed the conflict away from al Qaeda's favored "Sunnis vs. Americans and Shia" to a tribal conflict in which al Qaeda has no clear role. Also, the high entry costs of sectarian militias are likely to lead to two

---

[40] Eric Davis: "the overwhelming majority of those recruited to death squads in urban areas, for example, are rural to urban migrants. Yes, as you mentioned, they get some salary, they get a rifle, they get a uniform, they get the idea of belonging, protection from a group." http://www.pbs.org/newshour/bb/middle_east/july-dec06/iraq_10-30.html

favorable outcomes from al Qaeda's point of view—religious radicalization and deepening of sectarian identities. [41]

Sectarian militias, including al Qaeda, charged high entry costs in order to combat the "free rider" problem.[42] In order to form a cohesive organization, groups like al Qaeda need to shed the hangers-on, individuals who receive benefits from the group without contributing their share. Charging high entry costs both get rid of those individuals and bring the people who pay those costs closer together. In the case of al Qaeda, the price they charged was too high as their former tribal allies switched sides to work with the Americans. As mentioned earlier, tribes have the problem of involuntary membership, meaning a greater free rider problem and a decreased ability to charge high membership fees (as members are entitled to benefits based on kinship).

Groups providing security and social services will be able to charge prices at a level inverse to the degree of state failure (assuming weak or non-existent tribes, Iraqis will be forced to choose between sectarian militias and the state). As the official state falls further into collapse and is less able to provide security and social services, those public goods become more valuable and private providers such as sectarian militias are thus able to charge higher prices for them. The higher prices come in the form of more extreme religious policies—bans on smoking and alcohol, modest dress for women, etc. Higher entry prices will also lead to a greater degree of identification with the sect at the expense of the national identity. Obviously if the reverse happens and the state strengthens, security becomes less valuable and militias weaken as they can tt extract the same prices for their services.

---

[41] This is evident among Christians as well, as Christian militias spring up to defend enclaves of Iraqi Christians.
http://www.islamonline.net/servlet/Satellite?c=Article_C&cid=1216208140857&pagename=Zone-English-News/NWELayout
[42] For more on the "free rider" problem, see Iannacconne, *Religious Extremism*.

Religious radicalization worked for al Qaeda no matter what sect engaged in it. As Sunnis radicalized, they become ideologically closer to al Qaeda. When Shia groups radicalized, due to the cycle of violence between Sunni and Shia, they formed extremist identities in opposition to Sunni groups and were thus easier to exclude from al Qaeda's Islamic Caliphate identity. They also polarized identity politics.

As Iraqis fell back to tribal structures for security and social services and moved away from cooperation with al Qaeda, this presented an opportunity to American forces. Tribal forces were amenable to tactical alliances with coalition forces and also cut across sectarian identity. These tactical alliances pushed al Qaeda out of most areas in Iraq (as of early 2009). Tribal identities have historically existed within a broader Iraqi national identity, which would be concurrent with America's strategic goals in Iraq.

As Iraqi state structures collapsed, the coalition ended up partnering with Iraqi tribal leaders. Coalition forces and tribal forces together were eventually able to provide a basic level of security. Eventually the Iraqi state was able to rebuild both its military force (as evidenced by the Basra battle) and its social services.[43]

This analysis assumed that the leaders controlling al Qaeda pursued policies designed to advance the ideological goals of al Qaeda—i.e., creating a Islamic caliphate. But what if the organization you are trying to analyze does not have concrete identifiable goals, or is too loose-knit for a small group of decision makers to steer it in specific directions? This is when the unit of analysis shifts from an organization to a person.

---

[43] For instance see the statistics on electricity provisions in the Brookings Iraq Index:
http://www.brookings.edu/saban/~/media/Files/Centers/Saban/Iraq%20Index/index.pdf .

Many inner cities are plagued with violence, and much of this violence is related to gangs. Gang violence presents a different problem from violence in an insurgency—because there is less organization and no overarching political goal, gang violence can seem more senseless than political violence. However, many of the same dynamics that are present in insurgent violence also apply to gang violence. The lack of an organizing political goal mean that gangs are much easier to evaluate using the "natural systems" model of organizations, rather than the classical model as we analyzed al Qaeda in Iraq.

Rather than being senseless, gang violence can be viewed as a cost paid by individual gang members or wannabe members in order to receive goods from the gang. Most people are hard-wired against violence, [44] meaning the goods paid for by engaging in violence must be valuable.

The cost of violence includes the possibility of being caught by law enforcement and being punished, the cost of alienation from the community of law abiding citizens, as well as the psychological cost of engaging in personal violence. The possibility of punishment is the standard cost law enforcement attempts to impose on criminal behavior by deterrence, explained by Becker decades ago. [45] The deterrence against criminal behavior will be increased as both the punishment increases and as the likelihood of punishment increases.

Community alienation is also a cost of gang behavior; however this will vary widely by community and by individual. Some

---

[44] It is a "simple and demonstrable fact that there is within most men an intense resistance to killing their fellow man. A resistance so strong that, in many circumstances, soldiers on the battlefield will die before they can overcome it." Dave Grossman. *On Killing: The Psychological Cost of Learning to Kill in War and Society.* (Boston: Back Bay Books, 1996) at 4..

[45] Gary Becker. "Crime and Punishment: an Economic Approach." *The Journal of Political Economy.* 76:2, Mar 1968, pgs 169-217.

communities punish criminal behavior more than others, and many individuals are already alienated from their communities or families before gangs enter the picture. For example, the risk of gang membership for a family's son increases in "families where parents are less attached to their sons and do not supervise them very well" and where children are mistreated—i.e., where the individuals are already alienated (and thus the relative cost of gang membership is decreased).[46]

Another cost is the cognitive dissonance required to engage in violence against another human being. As Lt. Col. Dave Grossman writes in his book, when faced with a threat, individuals have a choice of four options: fight, posture, flight or submit. Fight, flight and submission have obvious meanings, and "posture" refers to acting as if one if fighting, but avoiding inflicting harm (for instance, deliberately firing over the enemy's head). Most individuals choose to not fight, even if it means they or their friends will be killed, unless they have undergone specific conditioning to enable them to kill.

Active gang membership can frequently mean dropping out or getting kicked out of school. This would seem to represent a major opportunity cost to gang membership. However, given the perception of poor employment prospects upon high school graduation, and poor college acceptance prospects, the cost of leaving school may not seem so high for many youths. Given the choice between making a few bucks on the corner today, and uncertain rewards far in the future, many people choose the immediate reward. And in broken families where parents are not able to force their children to go to school, that can be enough to make dropping out seem like the right decision.

---

[46] Terence Thornberry, Marvin Krohn, Alan Lizotte, Carolyn Smith, & Kimberly Tobin. "The Antecedents of Gang Membership." The Modern Gang Reader. (Los Angeles: Roxbury Publishing Company, 2006) at 36.

There are various ways to bring the "cost" of violence down. Grossman highlights the example of the crew-served machine gun as a way for individuals to rationalize that they are not in fact killing other human beings, but instead are performing their roles like cogs in a machine. Group involvement in violence distributes the responsibility (part of the cost) away from the individual and on to the group, meaning the cost to the individual is less and the benefits even greater (in terms of solidarity, friendship and prestige) as the act of committing group violence can not only function as a cost but also draws the gang members together.

The goods that gang members receive are non-monetary. Gang members typically don't make any money doing street-level drug sales. Instead, the benefits to gang membership are social, including friendship and social prestige, as well as physical protection. [47]

Youths are willing to pay the price of committing violence and running personal risk because of the environment in which gangs thrive. The absence of traditional suppliers (intact families, safe schools and neighborhoods, communities that are friendly to law enforcement) of protection, friendship, and other social goods creates a market for those goods, and gangs become one of many entrants into that market (along with community groups, churches, and other organizations).

Economic and rational choice analysis has gotten a bad rap in the past, largely because there have been a lot of bad rational

---

[47] "The Latin Kings are involved in drug trafficking, but most of the gang members are not in it for the money. They join for a sense of belonging and to protect themselves from other youths. They have little sense of history and often no idea why they fight, except to avenge slights, with rival gangs." W. Zachary Malinowski. "The Gangs of Providence: In the Renaissance City, the mean streets are what many youth call home." Providence Journal. February 8, 2008. Online at http://www.projo.com/news/content/GANGFINAL_07_02-10-08_E38oN7R_v105.1f15ddd.html .

choice analyses. For instance, Anatol Lieven has written "in Rational Choice theory... the default mode of humanity is to become Americans."[48] This is true of a lot of economic analysis, as an easy mistake to make is that of "mirror imaging", assuming the target of your analysis has the same goals, fears and incentives as you do. One example of this is the analysis leading up to the Iraq war. Because Americans desire a secular democratic republic, the Bush Administration assumed Iraqis desired the same thing.[49] This is why history and area studies become required reading for anyone attempting to address such problems. Unless the analyst understands both the environment in which their subject operates (institutions and constraints), as well as the goals and incentives of their subject, their conclusions will be flawed.

One of the advantages of economic analysis is that it leads naturally to policy prescriptions. If the starting assumption of economic analysis is that individuals make decisions under constraints and incentives, the next logical step is to adjust those constraints and incentives by altering policy. The two examples in this chapter both focused on sub-state organizations—various types of which are a growing concern both national and globally—that attempted to take advantage of market-like conditions. In both situations, the logical policy prescription would be to influence the actors indirectly by altering incentives and constraints, rather than applying a strategy that is focused solely on punishing the actors for filling a niche in the market. Unfortunately, in situations where there are serious negative aspects to the decisions made by the actors in questions, the logical prescription and the politically palatable one are rarely in synchronization. Therein lays the key to dealing with the seemingly irrational: implementing policy

---

[48] Anatol Lieven. *America Right or Wrong: An Anatomy of American Nationalism* at 66. (New York: Oxford University Press, 2004).
[49] Of course when this proved false, many of the same writers who predicted a welcoming response fell victim to Orientalism instead.

prescriptions that both treat the underlying disease and relieve the observable symptoms.

INFECTIOUS DISEASES, FOREIGN MILITARIES, AND US NATIONAL SECURITY

CHRISTOPHER ALBON

Militaries and infectious diseases have always been inexorably intertwined. History records hundreds of armies crippled by disease. In his account of the Peloponnesian War, Thucydides describes the devastation of a wartime plague on the Athenian people and leadership[50]. German General Erich Von Ludendorff blamed the 1918 Spanish flu pandemic for failure of his spring offensive and believed that it ultimately contributed to the Allied victory[51]. However, after World War II, the strategic implications of infectious disease on national security were overlooked. Instead the security and foreign policy communities primarily focused on the nuclear tension between the United States and the Soviet Union. National security under the Cold War paradigm was the "preservation of the state—its territorial integrity, political institutions, and national sovereignty—from physical threats"[52].

After the Cold War, attempts were made to expand the concept of security into new areas including economic, societal, and health security. The concept of human security has made particular headway. Human security was first posited in the 1994 United Nations *Human Development Report* and argues security must be redefined in terms of the individual rather than the state. The report lists a number of threats to individuals from famine to environmental destruction[53]. However, while human security's

---

[50] Thucydides. *The History of the Peloponnesian War: Revised Edition* at 151-156. (New York: Penguin Classics, 1954).
[51] Barry, John M. *The Great Influenza: The story of the deadliest pandemic in history* at 171. (New York: Penguin Books, 2005).
[52] Peterson, Susan. 2002. "Epidemic disease and national security." *Security Studies* 12(2) at 52
[53] United Nations Development Programme (1994): *Human Development Report*.

expanded definition has been useful, it is unnecessary in the present discussion. Infectious diseases are also threats in state-centric notion of national security. Diseases can weaken the capacity of militaries in developing states where the United States has significant national interest to respond to internal, external, and regional threats. Securing these states would place additional burden on the United States resources. The global risk from new and reemerging infectious diseases continue to rises in the 21st century and the disease burden placed on foreign militaries is a threat to United States national security.

THE GROWING IMPORTANCE OF INFECTIOUS DISEASES

The middle of the twentieth century saw rapid progress fighting various diseases[54]. Experts believed new technology had stemmed the spread of many infectious diseases in the developed world and lent hope of true worldwide health by the end of the millennium55. However, recently new infectious diseases have emerged and once controllable diseases have mutated and developed drug-resistance. Globalized trade, a growing and more mobile population, and widespread urbanization have resulted in emerging and reemerging infectious diseases spreading rapidly at the end of the 20th century[56.] This "third wave" of infectious diseases—including HIV, cholera, and tuberculosis—have become a significant threat[57]. The 2000 US National Intelligence Estimate[58] classified infectious disease for the first time as a threat to national security, warning, "new and reemerging infectious diseases will pose a rising global

---

[54] Noji, Eric K. 2001. "The Global Resurgence of Infectious Diseases." *Journal of Contingencies and Crisis Management* 9(4):223-232. Pg. 231.
[55] Peterson, Susan. 2002. "Epidemic disease and national security." *Security Studies* 12(2) at 47
[56] Noji, Eric K. 2001. "The Global Resurgence of Infectious Diseases." *Journal of Contingencies and Crisis Management* 9(4):223-232 at 225.
[57] Peterson, Susan. 2002. "Epidemic disease and national security." *Security Studies* 12(2). at 47.
[58] NIE 99-17D

health threat and will complicate US and global security"[59]. Infectious diseases in the future will thrive in an ever more interconnected, mobile, and crowded world.

The impact of infectious disease has struck hardest in the developing world, where poverty, conflict, and weak institutions leave states vulnerable. As a result, infectious diseases pose the greatest threat to developing states and their militaries. How might infectious diseases weaken the militaries of developing states? Where are they most vulnerable? To answer these questions, we examine a tragic and ongoing case study: HIV/AIDS in African militaries.

HIV/AIDS in African Armed Forces

Few doubt the devastating effect of HIV/AIDS on African militaries. African armed forces are "under direct attack from the disease"[60]. In 2007, around 22 million Africans were infected by the HIV-2 strain, representing two thirds of worldwide infections[61]. In seven Southern African states, HIV prevalence exceeds 15 percent[62].

Military personnel are at high risk of HIV infection. The majority of military personnel and recruits are between 18 and 24 years old and sexually actively[63]. Their elevated baseline risk is exacerbated by a military life of long deployments away from traditional social

---

[59] National Intelligence Council. 2000. "The Global Infectious Disease Threat and its Implications for the United States." Central Intelligence Agency. Online. Available: http://www.dni.gov/nic/special_globalinfectious.html (November 20, 2008).

[60] Singer, P. W. 2002. "AIDS and International Security." *Survival* 44(1):145-158.

[61] *Report on the global HIV/AIDS epidemic 2008.* (Geneva: Joint United Nations Programme on HIV/AIDS, 2008).

[62] *Report on the global HIV/AIDS epidemic 2008.* (Geneva: Joint United Nations Programme on HIV/AIDS, 2008).

[63] Fourie, P., and M. Schonteich. 2001. "Africa's New Security Threat: HIV and human security in Southern Africa." *African Security Review* 10(4):29-44.

networks and a military culture that promotes aggression, machismo, and risk taking[64].

The precise figure is debated but some armed forces are rumored to have HIV prevalence rates over 50 percent[65]. The South African National Defense Force (SANDF) admits between 10 and 12 percent of military personnel are HIV-positive, a range many consider conservative[66]. In 2004, China rejected one third of Zimbabwean officers for advanced training due to their HIV status[67]. HIV prevalence rates in African militaries are unknown or—in some cases—classified as state secrets[68]. However, it is reasonable to assume HIV rates are at least comparable to the state's civilian population and thus high enough to weaken African militaries in numerous ways.

Smaller Recruitment Pool—Recruits who are HIV-positive are seen as less suitable for military service. In response to high HIV prevalence in the general population some African militaries conduct pre-employment testing. However, testing can cause prospective recruits to self-select out of military service, shrinking the recruitment pool and reducing the overall quality of the armed forces.

Loss of Experienced Personnel—The effects of HIV/AIDS are felt all along the chain of command. Half of the Malawian general staff has been rumored to be HIV positive[69]. South Africa is facing rising

---

[64] Fourie, P., and M. Schonteich. 2001. "Africa's New Security Threat: HIV and human security in Southern Africa." *African Security Review* 10(4):29-44.
[65] Singer, P. W. 2002. "AIDS and International Security." *Survival* 44(1):145-158.
[66] Brower, Jennifer, and Peter Chalk. 2003. The Global Threat of New and Reemerging Infectious Diseases: Reconciling U.S. National Security and Public Health Policy. 1st ed. RAND Corporation.
[67] Garrett, Laurie. 2005. *HIV and National Security: Where are the Links?* Council on Foreign Relations.
[68] Tripodi, P., and P. Patel. 2004. "HIV/AIDS, Peacekeeping and Conflict Crises in Africa." *Medicine, Conflict and Survival* 20(3):195-208.
[69] Singer, P. W. 2002. "AIDS and International Security." *Survival* 44(1):145-158.

HIV prevalence in young blacks while 'fast tracking' young black officers into mid-level positions[70]. The Global Health Council predicts HIV/AIDS could deplete African armed forces of their senior personnel by 2012[71]. Experienced officers take decades to train and develop; they can be one of a military's most valuable resources. The loss of experienced personnel to HIV/AIDS erodes African militaries of their organizational capacity and institutional knowledge.

Reduction in Effectiveness—High infection rates weaken the ability of African militaries to operate effectively. Military personnel with AIDS are less able to complete physically demanding tasks[72], are more susceptible to adverse conditions during deployments[73], and have lower morale[74.] Furthermore, individuals unable to perform their duties must be transferred to less demanding roles, reducing the capacity of the military to deploy "homogenous" units[75].

Greater Financial Burden—African armed forces are primarily reliant on their human resources. However, eighty percent of beds in some African military hospitals are filled by AIDS patients[76]. The mounting financial costs of personnel with HIV/AIDS drains the

---

[70] Prins, Gwyn. 2004. "AIDS and global security." *International Affairs* 80(5):931-952.

[71] Sagala, John Kemoli. 2006. "HIV/AIDS and the Military in Sub-Saharan Africa: Impact on Military Organizational Effectiveness." *Africa Today* 53(1):53-77.

[72] Brower, Jennifer, and Peter Chalk. 2003. *The Global Threat of New and Reemerging Infectious Diseases: Reconciling U.S. National Security and Public Health Policy.* 1st ed. RAND Corporation.

[73] Heinecken, L. 2001. "Living in Terror: The looming security threat to Southern Africa." *African Security Review* 10(4):7-18.

[74] Tripodi, P., and P. Patel. 2004. "HIV/AIDS, Peacekeeping and Conflict Crises in Africa." *Medicine, Conflict and Survival* 20(3):195-208.

[75] Heinecken, L. 2001. "Living in Terror: The looming security threat to Southern Africa." *African Security Review* 10(4):7-18.

[76] Jackson J. Southern Africa AIDS Information Dissemination Service Bulletin, vol 4, No 2, adapted as: "The Quintessential AIDS in the Workplace Issue." In: *Civil-Military Alliance to Combat HIV and AIDS Newsletter,* October, 1996;4-7.

financial resources of African militaries. Militaries with high HIV prevalence have less financial resources available for their core functions. This has been called the "biggest challenge" for the SANDF[77].

Reduced Peacekeeping Capacity—HIV/AIDS weakens the ability of African armed forces to participate in regional peacekeeping operations. According to one account, at the start of the new millennium, the high prevalence of HIV in African armed forces hampered the United Nations' capacity to fulfill the demand for peacekeepers on the continent[78]. The epidemic undermines peacekeeping capacity in three ways. First, HIV/AIDS is making states reluctant to contribute peacekeepers. One study found HIV prevalence amongst peacekeepers in Sierra Leone rose from 7% to 15% during a three-year deployment[79]. Faced with the positive correlation between peacekeeping and HIV prevalence, Africa states are less willing to contribute forces to peacekeeping operations[80]. Second, high HIV prevalence reduces the ability of African armed forces to deploy peacekeepers. The combination of a high HIV-prevalence amongst SANDF personnel and a policy of excluding HIV-positive troops from U.N. peacekeeping duty means that up to a significant portion of troops are unavailable for deployment[81]. One South African official reportedly claimed that

---

[77] Heinecken, L. 2001. "Living in Terror: The looming security threat to Southern Africa." *African Security Review* 10(4):7-18.

[78] General Accounting Office. 2001. *UN Peacekeeping: United Nations Faces Challenges in Responding to the Impact of HIV/AIDS on Peacekeeping Operations. Report to the Chairman, Committee on International Relations, House of Representatives.* GAO–02–194.

[79] Feldbaum, Harley, Kelley Lee, and Preeti Patel. 2006. "The National Security Implications of HIV/AIDS." *PLoS Medicine* 3(6):e171 EP -.

[80] Feldbaum, Harley, Kelley Lee, and Preeti Patel. 2006. "The National Security Implications of HIV/AIDS." *PLoS Medicine* 3(6):e171 EP -.

[81] Brower, Jennifer, and Peter Chalk. 2003. *The Global Threat of New and Reemerging Infectious Diseases: Reconciling U.S. National Security and Public Health Policy.* 1st ed. RAND Corporation.

HIV/AIDS was the primary reason South Africa has not been more involved in the conflict in the Democratic Republic of the Congo[82].

IMPLICATIONS FOR US NATIONAL SECURITY

The specific effects and risks to a nation's military are unique to individual infectious diseases. However, the case of HIV/AIDS in African armed forces offers general insights into the potential effects of infectious diseases on the militaries of developing nations and the implications for United States national security.

Infectious diseases can threaten the domestic security and stability of developing nations where the United States has significant national interest. Armed forces are often called upon to maintain domestic security. Militaries crippled by HIV/AIDS are less able operate in this capacity. Governments unable to maintain domestic security could be perceived as less legitimate by the civilian population and increase popular support for non-state armed opposition groups. Thus, the demands placed on armed forces to protect against domestic threats would be likely negatively related to the military's own effectiveness[83].

Militaries of developing nations heavily burdened by infectious diseases are vulnerable to external threats. Regional stability is maintained by a balance of power. Shifts in the power dynamic amongst states increase the risk of interstate war. Militaries of developing nations weakened by infectious diseases are less able to deter international aggression. Even the perception of security vulnerability from infectious diseases could trigger opportunistic

---

[82] Brower, Jennifer, and Peter Chalk. *The Global Threat of New and Reemerging Infectious Diseases: Reconciling U.S. National Security and Public Health Policy.* (Santa Monica: RAND Corporation, 2003).

[83] Moodie, M., and W. J. Taylor. 2000. *Contagion and Conflict—Health as a Global Security Challenge. Report of the Chemical and Biological Arms Control Institute and the CSIS International Security Programs.* (Washington, D.C.: Center for Strategic and International Studies, 2000).

invasion[84]. The United States has an interest in maintaining regional stability, not only for normative reasons, but also to protect strategic or economic US national interests in the area.

Infectious diseases could limit a state's capacity to conduct peacekeeping operations. States with militaries debilitated by infectious diseases would be less able to muster an effective peacekeeping force from their reduced ranks. Even if a military had the capacity to contribute peacekeepers, the state might be reluctant to deploy them and stretch their already thinning ranks. Furthermore, states hosting peacekeeping forces could resist the presence of infected troops and the resultant risk of spreading the disease to their citizens[85]. As infectious diseases reduce a state's peacekeeping capacity the burden could increasingly fall on the United States and its western allies to maintain regional stability or risk wider conflicts.

INFECTIOUS DISEASE AND US NATIONAL SECURITY POLICY

In the 21st century, infectious diseases are increasingly a serious threat to the national security of the United States, even if they strike outside the nation's borders. The lessons learned from the effect of HIV/AIDS in African militaries reveal the necessity of giving health concerns a more central position in discussions of national security. In particular, US programs to strengthen the effectiveness of developing world security forces must also increase their health capacity. The United States has a national security interest in strengthening the capacity of friendly foreign armed forces to respond to infectious diseases within their ranks. The framework for this program already exists. The United States' African Contingency Operations Training and Assistance program

---

[84] International Crisis Group, *HIV/AIDS as a Security Issue* (Washington, DC: International Crisis Group, 2001

[85] Ban, J. 2003. "Health as a global security challenge." *Seton Hall Journal of Diplomacy and International Relations* 4(2):19-28.

boosts the capacity of African militaries to conduct peacekeeping and humanitarian missions on the continent. The program's greatest challenge, according to one commentator, is that the HIV/AIDS epidemic is crippling the participating militaries before they can be effectively deployed[86]. Enlarging the role of health capacity building in this and similar programs offers a means to make friendly militaries more resistant to infectious disease, increasing their ability to provide domestic, international, and regional stability.

---

[86] Singer, P. W. 2002. "AIDS and International Security." *Survival* 44(1):145-158.

PAKISTAN AS A NUCLEAR RISK

STEVE SCHIPPERT

Ask any reasonably informed American news consumer about Iran and they will instinctively bring up the Iranian nuclear threat. Likewise, ask about the threat emanating from Pakistan, and they will likely mention terrorism, specifically al Qaeda, the Taliban and their havens of operation in the "wild west" tribal areas. While these threats certainly exist regarding Iran and Pakistan, the threat perception with each is unfortunately inverted.

Iran has yet to develop a nuclear weapon. And while the prospects for such development grow direr with each passing month of uninhibited development of the Iranian nuclear weapons program, little short of a rogue nuclear weapons purchase is likely to change Iran's nuclear arms status in the short term.

The principal threat from Iran at current is that of terrorism. Iran is today the foremost state sponsor of international terrorism and has been since its 1979 Islamic revolution, which ushered in a thuggish theocracy, violent and murderous both within and without its borders. It created the Islamic Revolutionary Guard Corps (IRGC), whose Quds Force holds as its primary mission "exporting the revolution" beyond Iranian borders.

The Quds Force "export" of the Iranian revolution can be most readily seen today in the funding, training, grooming and arming of terrorist groups such as Hizballah in Lebanon, Hamas and other terrorist groups in the Palestinian territories, and Iraqi insurgents, militias and "Special Groups." Israeli civilians and soldiers alike are the regular targets of such terrorist groups. In Iraq, according to statistics released by the Department of Defense, over 10% of all US casualties in Iraq have come at the hands of Explosively Formed Projectile (EFP) roadside bombs. These are of Iranian design and Iran has supplied Iraqi groups the weapons as well as the training, hardware and technology to manufacture and assemble them locally. The 10% figure represents EFP fatalities alone, and does not include US casualties caused by the use of other weapons and ammunition supplied by Iran.

Iran has persistently conducted terrorist operations internationally since the 1983 bombings of the US Marine barracks, American embassy and French paratrooper barracks in Beirut. Yet, the high-profile crisis surrounding the advancing Iranian nuclear program has had an undeniable effect of back-seating their current and historical sponsorship of terrorism in the minds of the American public.

Pakistan, on the other hand, has an arsenal of nuclear weapons on hand. There are two key differences between Pakistan and Iran surrounding this critical distinction.

The first distinction is that, unlike Iran, Pakistan as a state is not a threat in the manner that Iran is as a state sponsor of terrorism. While our friends in India may take an understandably different view, there is a larger distinction between a border conflict between to neighboring states and the export of terrorism far beyond those borders as Iran does with Hizballah and Hamas.

The second distinction is that Iran is not actively combating a destabilizing insurgency within its own borders. The Pakistani state is under siege from al Qaeda, the Taliban and other aligned terrorist groups. It is a slow-motion insurgency being patiently executed within the framework of a 'death by a thousand cuts' strategy. Various peace accords agreed to by the previous Musharraf government have ceded significant swaths of Pakistani territory to the Taliban-al Qaeda alliance, affording the terrorists safe haven in exchange for fleeting Pakistani relief from military engagement. The Pakistani military has remained engaged, particularly so since early 2008 under General Kiyani. The results are mixed, however. It has seen gains in some places, stalemate in others, and not insignificant losses elsewhere. The Taliban-al Qaeda alliance insurgency continues apace.

While the object of the insurgency is to acquire the levers of power and resources of a state, Pakistan is the al Qaeda focus for two reasons: proximity of their organization's power and influence and—most notably—Pakistan's nuclear arsenal. Should they ultimately achieve their aims, many may not immediately notice exactly what has happened.

al Qaeda will not take to flying their black banner of jihad over Islamabad's institutions should they gain significant control and influence. Instead, the Pakistani government will be run by Pakistani allies with at least a degree of perceived separation between the Taliban-al Qaeda alliance and these political and military leaders.

Nawaz Sharif, according to Michael Scheuer, former head of the CIA's bin Laden desk, was reported in the Pakistani press to have received billions of rupees from Usama bin Laden "[b]efore the elections in 1990, bin Laden's family and friends gave Nawaz Sharif one billion rupees." Benazir Bhutto had claimed that bin Laden had funded a failed attempt at a no-confidence vote against her and her government through Nawaz Sharif. Scheuer notes that while there is no hard evidence that bin Laden gave such sums to Bhutto's political rival, note that it is true, quoting bin Laden himself, that unlike Bhutto, Nawaz Sharif "always played an exemplary role in the Afghan jihad." [87]

He and his party, the Pakistani Muslim League—Nawaz (PML-N)—now share significant power with the late Benazir Bhutto's Pakistani Peoples' Party (PPP) and the current president, Bhutto's widow Asif Ali Zardari. While Nawaz Sharif is not an al Qaeda "true

---

[87] Michael Scheuer, Through Our Enemies' Eyes: Osama bin Laden, Radical Islam, and the Future of America, (Dulles, Virginia: Potomac Books, 2002), 176

believer" by any stretch, he is a political being who takes support for his ambitions wherever he finds it. Follow his words carefully and one will never hear Nawaz Sharif criticize the Taliban or al Qaeda. This is in line with bin Laden's direct praise for the Pakistani politician. Biting the hand that feeds is not in Nawaz Sharif's political cards. That said, Nawaz Sharif would surely have a short shelf-life of usefulness for al Qaeda should they attain the goals and assume significant control.

Such cannot be said of former ISI director and retired Pakistani general, Hamid Gul. He is often referred to as the "godfather of the Taliban," having played a significant role in its creation while heading the ISI. He is a friend of bin Laden, though he works hard to maintain the perception of a degree of separation. In the wake of the Mumbai terrorist attack that dragged on violently from November 26-29, 2008, India demanded his arrest and extradition for involvement in the planning of the attack. He nevertheless wields significant power within Pakistani political and intelligence circles.

In an October 2001 conversation with respected journalist and Washington Times and United Press International editor at large, Arnaud de Borchgrave, "Gen. Gul forecast a future [Pakistani] Islamist nuclear power that would form a greater Islamic state with a fundamentalist Saudi Arabia after the monarchy falls." [88] This is precisely the danger that al Qaeda poses in Pakistan, with the assistance of powerful Pakistani military and intelligence allies like Hamid Gul. This very real and present danger is precisely why Pakistan—and not Iran—poses a greater nuclear risk than Iran.

The 9/11 Commission Report stated that after the August 1998 cruise missile strike that "missed bin Laden by a few hours,"

---

[88] Arnaud de Borchgrave , "Report: Pakistan's ISI 'Fully Involved' in 9/11," *Newsmax,* August 4, 2004

Washington officials "speculated that one or another Pakistani official might have sent a warning to the Taliban or bin Laden." [89] The Christian Science Monitor was more specific, reporting that in the Commission's meetings "[e]vidence emerged" that "former Pakistani intelligence chief, Hamid Gul, forewarned bin Laden of the 1998 missile strikes so that he was able to escape."[90] Following the 2003 invasion of Iraq, Gul said that "God will destroy the U.S. in Iraq and Afghanistan and wherever it will try to go from there." Calling U.S. actions a "war against Muslims," he added, "Let's destroy America wherever its troops are trapped." Hamid Gul is also said to be friends with Mullah Omar, the Taliban leader.

These are the two most notable al Qaeda allies within Pakistan, who provide the public face of al Qaeda with a degree of plausible deniability—although their neutrality is given credence only by those who seek conflict avoidance at any cost. It may also be prudent to consider among them Abdul Qadeer Khan, the immensely popular Pakistani nuclear scientist and black marketer known as the "Father of the Islamic Bomb." He is, at minimum, sympathetic to al Qaeda and the Taliban and maintains ire toward the Pakistani government. His popularity as a symbol of Pakistani national pride would serve al Qaeda's aims or proffering a fellow traveler as leader while maintaining the desired perception of a degree of separation.

But there can be little doubt that Nawaz Sharif is bought and paid for political goods, a "useful idiot" (in Stalin's phrase) in the eyes of al Qaeda. And he would likely serve as a temporary leadership bridge ultimately to Hamid Gul, who is not a useful idiot for al Qaeda nor simply sympathetic to them, but rather a true believer.

---

[89] National Commission on the Terrorist Attacks Upon the United States, *9/11 Commission Report* (Washington DC: GPO, 2004), 117
[90] David Montero, "More evidence of Taliban leader hiding in Pakistan," *Christian Science Monitor*, January 19, 2007.

And within the context of Gul's statement envisioning "a future [Pakistani] Islamist nuclear power that would form a greater Islamic state with a fundamentalist Saudi Arabia," your author concluded in a September 2008 analysis that this is "the al Qaeda progression. Nothing assures its completion, but little impedes it from within Pakistan. "[91]

To evaluate the level of threat or risk posed by or from Pakistan and Iran, a simple mathematical equation can be used to arrive at a basic understanding and assessment of corresponding urgency.

Risk/Threat = Likelihood X Consequences

Considering the nuclear risks, the consequences of the Iranian state possessing a nuclear weapon are grave. The argument is often made addressing likelihood is that Iran would act relatively reasonably because it has a state to preserve. This argument may hold some validity among certain Iranian leaders, but it discounts the messianic nature of the regime itself, evidenced by Mahmoud Ahmadinejad's repeated calls to "pave the way for the return of the Hidden (12th) Imam."

In Shi'a faith espoused by the Iranian regime, the 12th Imam's return will occur only when the world is embroiled within unprecedented death, war, destruction and violence. And it is within this context that "paving the way," as envisioned by Ahmadinejad and his powerful and equally messianic spiritual mentor Ayatollah Mezbah Yazdi, differs sharply from the Christian belief that one should "be prepared" spiritually and personally because man will "know neither the day nor the hour" of the return of Jesus Christ. Both events represent for their faith's days of judgment and salvation. But, considering the pretext required,

---

[91] Steve Schippert, "al Qaeda's Progression On Pakistan's Demise: Schizophrenic Pakistan And The Coming Vacuum That Invites al Qaeda," *ThreatsWatch.org*, September 8, 2008

nuclear weapons in the hands of those who believe they must "pave the way" by realizing that pretext would increase the likelihood of their use and the grave consequences that would result.

But Iran has yet to achieve nuclear weapons production, making the current likelihood assessment—for the moment—quite low in the risk equation.

Regarding the risk posed by Pakistan's nuclear arsenal, the consequences of their use are equally grave. But the likelihood side of the equation hinges not on the state of Pakistan, but rather on the potential for the Taliban-al Qaeda gaining control of them. Nuclear weapons in the hands of al Qaeda pose a greater risk than those in the hands of Iran, for there is no plausible argument that the terrorists would hesitate to use them against its enemies, including the West and, notably, India. To that end, the state of Pakistan holds its nuclear arsenal as a defensive deterrent guarantee against bordering rival India. Al Qaeda, on the other hand, seeks to destroy its enemies rather than defend territory. Offense is its defense, and for this principal reason, among others, the likelihood of a nuclear detonation with al Qaeda controlling nuclear weapons is far greater than that of any state, even including Iran.

The question then remains today not one of the likelihood of al Qaeda employing nuclear weapons, but rather the likelihood of al Qaeda actually attaining them. It lacks the means to produce, with resources required necessarily limited to those of a functioning state (or, in the case of North Korea, a quasi-functioning state with resources allocated at all costs.) al Qaeda must acquire nuclear weapons, either by rogue purchase or by force.

It is not by mistake or pure happenstance that al Qaeda, allied with the various Pakistani Taliban groups, has constituted an insurgency within Pakistan. There is a reason it fights much harder inside Pakistan when pressed than it does even in Afghanistan. The

Afghanistan campaign, while not without genuine intentions, is largely for greater international public consumption. The prize is Pakistan, for its resources and capabilities beyond the reach of a stateless terrorist organization. And while it hopes to co-opt the Pakistani military and intelligence resources and structures, the crown jewel is the Pakistani nuclear arsenal.

In fact, because of the nature of the Pakistani nuclear arsenal, al Qaeda cannot take Pakistan by pure brute force. It must co-opt significant portions of the Pakistani military and intelligence institutions. With warhead and delivery vehicles stored in binary fashion (separately, unassembled) as well as the multiple electronic key code security layers in place for arming them , al Qaeda requires those with access and technical operating skills to join them—or at least assist or not obstruct them. al Qaeda already has a measure of supporters within the Pakistani military and military intelligence (ISI), and a greater number who are at least sympathetic.

It is because of al Qaeda's need to topple the Pakistani government with its military and intelligence intact that it has executed two different approaches to its insurgency. The approach applied to the professional Pakistani military is a psychological operation (PSYOP) intended to convince the somewhat younger ranks, more easily influenced and less exposed to Western military ties, to "come back to Islam" and embrace the jihad. While an attempt to actively recruit members from within the Pakistani military, this also serves to "soften the landing,," so to speak, and fertilize the fields for less resistance and increased acquiescence once al Qaeda, by its designs, topples the Pakistani government and asserts its own degrees of expanded control.

The approach al Qaeda has applied to the less professional paramilitary units employed against them and the Taliban consists of little careful PSYOP. Instead, armed members of the Frontier

Corps are confronted with the violence and lethality of warfare without hesitation. Rather than co-opting the Frontier Corps (FC), which is more localized and far less well trained and equipped than the regular Pakistani military, al Qaeda and the Taliban have taken to infiltrating its units, with local Pakistanis aligned or sympathetic to the terrorists joining the Crops' ranks as volunteers. This affords them significant intelligence on operations and pending operations against the Taliban and al Qaeda in hot regions such as North and South Waziristan, Bajaur, and others where they have been directly confronted. The terrorists use this intelligence not to co-opt them, but to kill them, often in gruesome manners intended to send an intimidating message back to surviving FC members, the local Pakistani people and the rest of the world.

From 2007 through the summer of 2008, the situation in Pakistan looked increasingly bleak. The government of Pakistan was disintegrating with Pervez Musharraf's relentless cling to power followed by his eventual fall after the early 2008 elections. The newly elected coalition government led by bitter rivals Zardari (PPP) and Nawaz Sharif (PML-N) seemed incapable of coalition, let alone actual governance, and Pakistan had never before seemed so unstable, teetering on the edge of collapse. The situation for the Pakistani government stabilized somewhat in the last five months of 2008, though this is not to say that Pakistan approaches anything resembling stability. It does demonstrate, however, a distinct decrease in the likelihood of the Taliban-al Qaeda alliance's momentum carrying them into greater control and power following a once nearly imminent collapse of the Pakistani government, as it had once seemed quite possible.

The threat remains, and the consequences of al Qaeda's acquisition of nuclear weapons are persistently grave. The al Qaeda insurgency continues and the quest for the acquisition of Pakistan and her nuclear arsenal as the cornerstone for the creation of bin Laden's and Ayman al-Zawahiri's envisioned caliphate has not ended. The insurgency itself remains strong, though the government of Pakistan seems to have shored up some significant weaknesses. But the decrease in the terrorists' momentum, for the moment at least, subsequently also decreases the likelihood of al Qaeda seizing control of much of Pakistan and her nuclear arsenal. This could change rapidly with unforeseen events, such as an open war between the Indian and Pakistani states and the instability the prospects of a Pakistani defeat would bring.

What does all this mean for the United States going forward, particularly as a new administration takes custody of the levers of American power? It means that as the military and intelligence focus begins to shift to Afghanistan, success there is inextricably linked directly to Pakistan. Whatever bleeding occurs in Afghanistan, the wound and source is and has been all along inside Pakistani territory.

With Robert Gates remaining as Secretary of Defense and General David Petraeus overseeing the theater and region at CENTCOM, a vexing situation is placed in the hands of a smart and reliable command. They can be expected to be afforded most theater decision making power with little interference or public dissent from the Obama administration. If they are successful, the sitting president is afforded credit as Commander in Chief. If the situation deteriorates, they can be politically dismissed as George W. Bush's men.

There remain two primary challenges regarding the Taliban-al Qaeda alliance (and affiliated groups such as Lashkar-e-Taiba) operating from within Pakistan. The first challenge is still confronting them and defeating them in place. This entails killing or capturing its fighters and commanders, disrupting their financial networks and their recruiting and radicalization efforts, and ultimately driving a wedge between the terrorists and the local populations. The latter aspect of the military challenge necessarily requires Pakistani military forces doing the heavy lifting for the former.

The second challenge is as much a matter of diplomatic efforts as it is one of military and intelligence. The November 26-29 terrorist attacks in Mumbai, India, brought from the shadows to the forefront the need to prevent a hot conventional war between the Indian and Pakistani states. The Mumbai attack was designed to spark an Indian military retaliation within Pakistani territory, igniting another war between the two rivals. Pakistan would then be forced to withdraw its army from engagements with the Taliban and al Qaeda in the Federally Administered Tribal Areas (FATA) and the NorthWest Frontier Province (NWFP) in order to concentrate forces for defensive and offensive operations along the Indian border. This would not only provide a much needed reprieve for the terrorists and the immediate restoration of the safety of their carved sanctuaries, it would also create increased instability within the rest of Pakistan as well as India. And state instability is for a terrorist group what fertilizer is for a fresh spring lawn.

Should terrorist groups successfully spark a war between India and Pakistan, then the likelihood multiplier in the Risk/Threat = Likelihood X Consequences formula skyrockets regarding the risk to Pakistan's nuclear arsenal. And those who sought to achieve this through the Mumbai attacks will try again and again until they succeed in wearing down Indian patience and successfully elicit a retaliatory attack. Such prospects have little to do with our success against the Taliban, al Qaeda and aligned groups—unless we (to rightfully and necessarily include Pakistan) defeat them largely in place.

But time is not our friend. It is far easier and exponentially less time consuming for a group to plan and execute more terrorist attacks inside India than it is for us to defeat them. India may respond militarily after another similar attack by terrorists from within Pakistan, sparking the state-on-state Indo-Pak war the terrorists are seeking for their own relief. And this prospect of volatility and instability is precisely what makes the Pakistani nuclear arsenal a greater risk than the Iranian arsenal that is still being researched and has yet to be fielded.

NUCLEAR NONPROLIFERATION IN THE 21ST CENTURY

CHERYL ROFER AND MOLLY CERNICEK

Almost two decades after the dissolution of the Soviet Union, nuclear weapons policy seems stuck in the Cold War. The standoff of mutually assured destruction (MAD) is no longer a staple of diplomacy, but the missiles remain on alert. Weapons have been disassembled, but pits remain in storage, ready in case of a dustup requiring several thousands of them.

Meanwhile, the world has changed around those nuclear arsenals. Although the United States and Russia are unlikely to incinerate each other, India and Pakistan may yet give us nuclear winter. More likely are accidents involving the launch of those missiles on alert or the handling of the remaining nuclear weapons. Material and weapons remain incompletely secured from theft, and the development of the A. Q. Khan network has increased the possible sources of materials and weapons for non-state actors. Many US government functions have been privatized, including some previously carried out by the military and the management of all aspects of the nuclear weapons complex, opening the question of distortions in government policy in response to the need for private profit.

The Nuclear Nonproliferation Treaty has been immensely successful. All nations but three (India, Israel and Pakistan) have signed it, and only one (North Korea) has withdrawn from it. Those four all have nuclear weapons, for a total of nine nuclear weapons nations in a world that once was expected to have dozens. Despite success, some work remains undone. Article IV allows the full nuclear fuel cycle to any nation for peaceful use, but the fuel cycle puts a nation within shouting distance of a nuclear weapon. Article VI promises that the nuclear weapon nations will work toward nuclear and general disarmament; whether they have lived up to their commitment remains contentious.

Because so few nations possess nuclear weapons, and the United States and Russia possess overwhelming numbers of them, their policies are key to the future of nonproliferation. The for-profit sector, including the A. Q. Khan network, has also become a significant factor.

NATIONAL THREATS

The national threats are related to the existing nuclear arsenals, the nascent arsenal in North Korea, and the question of Iran's intentions. Each nation poses distinctive threats.

National threats in the established nuclear nations (United States, Russia, United Kingdom, France, China, Israel, India and Pakistan) have to do largely with accidental launch of nuclear missiles or other accidents regarding the handling of nuclear weapons and components. The United States and Russia maintain land-based missiles on alert. Such missiles are the most vulnerable of the nuclear delivery vehicles, and their use requires rapid decisions, before an adversary can destroy them. In fixed locations, they are much more vulnerable than submarine- or bomber-delivered weapons. An accidental launch or false alarm thus could provoke a nuclear exchange.

Two recent incidents in the United States illustrate other sorts of accidents. Six nuclear weapons were inadvertently affixed to bombers transiting between Minot and Barksdale Air Force bases. They were unguarded for 36 hours while the planes sat on the tarmac. And nuclear weapon components were accidentally shipped to Taiwan by the US military because of a parts number mix-up. Both incidents opened the weapons and their components to theft and misuse. Russia's nuclear handling practices are unlikely to be any better.

India and Pakistan present the most likely scenario for the military use of nuclear weapons. Relations between the two countries are tense, in part over the territory of Kashmir, but have the potential to improve through actions such as Pakistan's recent approval to allow foreign direct investment from India. Both countries suffer terror attacks, most recently in Mumbai and Karachi, which could spark a nuclear confrontation. An exchange of several tens of nuclear weapons between these two countries could cause a nuclear winter.[92] Pakistan's instability and infiltration by the Taliban are of concern in case of a failure of the national government, in which case nuclear weapons could fall into the hands of the Taliban or other subnational groups. Current rumor has it that Pakistan's nuclear weapons have now been fitted with permissive action links to make them difficult or impossible for unauthorized use.

Israel is believed to have about 200 nuclear weapons, although its official policy and that of its allies, most notably the United States, is not to admit that this is the case. This awkward and dangerous situation has historical roots[93] but hinders progress toward peace between Israel and its neighbors. For example, Arab states continue to propose a nuclear weapons free zone in the Middle East, but the proposal goes nowhere partly because it is an attempt on the part of the Arab states to goad Israel into an admission of its nuclear arsenal, and partly because Israel and the United States act to block it so that Israel may maintain its nuclear monopoly in the region. This discussion is masked, however. Such inability to face this problem is also a difficulty in all negotiations between Israel and its neighbors.

---

[92] Owen B. Toon, Alan Robock, Richard P. Turco, Charles Bardeen, Luke Oman, and Georgiy I. Stenchikov, "Consequences of Regional-Scale Nuclear Conflicts," *Science* **315**, 1224-1225 (2 March 2007).
[93] Avner Cohen, *Israel and the Bomb* (New York: Columbia University Press, 1998).

Although North Korea appears to have enough plutonium for perhaps a dozen weapons, it is not clear how many they have manufactured. Their underground test of October 2006 had a very low yield and may well have been a nuclear fizzle, indicating a poor design or manufacture. Six-party talks continue with many ups and downs in the negotiations, but it appears likely that some agreement will eventually be reached.

Iran claims that its development of a nuclear fuel cycle is for civilian use only, but the capability it is building will very likely support the manufacture of nuclear weapons. Combined with a lack of candor about earlier experiments and some recent developments, this development raises questions as to whether Iran's goal is to be able to produce nuclear weapons on short notice while maintaining its fuel cycle primarily for civilian purposes. Its facilities are regularly inspected by the International Atomic Energy Agency (IAEA), which would report any irregularities pointing to weapons development. Negotiations are also under way between Iran and European countries to ensure that its program remains civilian.

The greatest danger of nuclear proliferation lies in the uncontrolled acquisition of nuclear arsenals by North Korea or Iran. In the case of North Korea, Japan and South Korea would be inclined to develop nuclear weapons capability. Both have the technological base to do this in short order. In the case of Iran, given that, in the area, Israel, India and Pakistan already have nuclear weapons capability; many other states in western Asia would be inclined toward acquiring nuclear weapons capability. None are as technologically advanced as Japan and South Korea, but several have made public an interest in acquiring all or part of the nuclear fuel cycle.

THE PRIVATIZATION OF NUCLEAR WEAPONS MANUFACTURE

During the last two decades, nuclear weapons manufacture has slipped into the private sector. This development is less understood and less amenable to the previous treaty-based means of controlling the spread of nuclear weapons.

The A. Q Khan network has not been fully unfolded. However, it is clear that numerous individuals and businesses acted independently and in cooperation to produce some of the highly-specialized components necessary for producing nuclear weapons. Identifying, tracking and destroying elements of the network have generated questions involving state credibility, NPT signatories' responsibilities, and sovereignty.

As an example, a father and sons, Friedrich, Marco and Urs Tinner of Switzerland, were suspected of supplying key technology for uranium enrichment to Libya's nuclear weapons program as well as other dealings through the Khan network from 2001 to 2003. In 2004, all three were arrested in Switzerland (Urs Tinner was extradited from Germany) on suspicion of violating export laws on controlled goods and war materials. Critical evidence surrounding this case was destroyed by the Swiss government in late 2007 or in 2008.[94]

Questions remain as to who requested the destruction of the files—the IAEA as a signatory requirement under the NPT, or the Swiss federal government at the request of the CIA. Why were the documents destroyed instead of being transferred to the IAEA for study and safe-keeping? What was the relationship between the CIA and the Tinner family members between 2003 and 2007? After almost four years of pretrial detention, Urs Tinner has been

---

[94] "Did Switzerland Give in to US Pressure?" Swissinfo.ch, May 30, 2008. http://www.swissinfo.org/eng/front/Did_Switzerland_give_in_to_US_pressure.html?siteSect=105&sid=9152887&cKey=1214213289000&ty=st

released,[95] while his brother Marco remains in detention. Without documentation and without trials, the Tinners cannot present their defense.

Should the Swiss government allow them to face trials, information surrounding their proliferation activities and possible intelligence cooperation could reach the public domain. Some Swiss legislators have requested a parliamentary investigation to determine whether the Federal Council violated the separation of powers, whereas others consider the destruction of documents necessary to national and international security. This kind of scenario could very well become more typical and demands additional coordination and tactics to ensure continued cooperation between nonproliferation stakeholders.

Another sort of privatization, more public and less sinister, has been taking place in the American nuclear complex. Privatization of the management is now complete, including the Los Alamos and Livermore design laboratories. This model adds additional players and interests to the process of nuclear weapons policy.

A common perception is that private companies are more efficient, cost-effective, innovative and flexible than government organizations. Yet market forces work poorly under monopolistic conditions, which is the case for the nuclear weapons design laboratories. A company's efficiency is only in regards to making profit for the company's shareholders, not to save taxpayer money or to outperform government employees. A company can be profitable without being efficient, especially when it lacks competitors and has a contracted long-term customer. A company prefers to utilize its infrastructure and its corporate knowledge base to sell its services or products, not to risk a large investment on retooling and refocusing its business model unless there is no other choice. A company may prefer to fail rather than to implement a new business plan.

The major products of the nuclear weapons complex are nuclear weapons design, development, maintenance, intelligence and nonproliferation. The contractors have a strong incentive to convince the National Nuclear Security Administration (NNSA) and lobby Congress to allocate resources to continue the existing business model. It would be extraordinarily risky for any of these contractors to lobby the Congress and the Department of Energy for funding to create product lines and infrastructure in an area that may have a future, but has received no significant government funding to date—such as energy security. The current private contractors struggle to attract funds for new and innovative research outside of the Department of Energy. The management vision and oversight required to implement transformation would eat into the management bonus fees received each year and paid to shareholders.

Leadership and direction for a modern mission in nuclear weapons as well as prioritizing and supporting research is the function of government, not its profit-making contractors. Transforming the broad and substantial scientific and engineering resources of the nuclear weapons complex will take extraordinary vision and commitment by individuals and organizations who have a different viewpoint from the lobbyists of private contractors. The numbers and missions of nuclear weapons should be decided only on the basis of international threats and the foreign policy of the United States, not on the basis of profit motive, shareholder interest, and professional relationships. The United States government has an opportunity now to reduce world tensions, the risk of nuclear weapons use, the development of a nuclear weapons based marketplace, and the risk of terrorists getting hold of materials by moving toward further arms control initiatives aggressively. But the US Congress and government must be committed to changing the contractor model as presently practiced.

ARE NUCLEAR WEAPONS TOO DANGEROUS TO USE?

The nations possessing nuclear weapons justify their arsenals in terms of deterrence and the possibility that wartime circumstances might require their use. But we simply don't know how or whether deterrence works in a multipolar world. The moves were worked out in great detail for the two-player deterrence of the Cold War; but game theory and physics tell us that problems involving many players or bodies become so much more complicated that they may not be amenable to analysis. No Herman Kahn has arisen in the 21st century to analyze potential moves and countermoves. A rough-and-ready sort of deterrence exists in that nations try not to attack others that are more armed than themselves, but conventional weapons can also play this role.

Nuclear weapons have never been used in war since their first use on Japan in 1945. Thomas Schelling attributes this to a "nuclear taboo."[96] Their nonuse has also been attributed to the deterrence of their possession by other nations. The immensely destructive power of nuclear weapons makes them difficult to use in warfare. Potential political, social and geological consequences have also forced governments to draw back from their use. As noted above, an exchange of several tens of nuclear weapons could bring about nuclear winter for the entire globe. Economic damage from a lesser attack could also damage the aggressor as well as the victim.

The global economy has changed substantially since the first use of nuclear weapons. Today, there exists a substantial risk of a global economic panic and shattered investor confidence in any region where a nuclear weapon is detonated, or perhaps even attempted.

---

[96] Thomas C. Schelling, "The Nuclear Taboo," *MIT International Review* 1(1), Spring 2007 http://web.mit.edu/mitir/2007/spring/taboo.html

Not only would there be infrastructural damages, substantial losses to financial assets and currency devaluation, but also investment would be withdrawn from a victimized region, country, or countries. Investors, pension plans and customers relying on a victimized country's services, products, and profits would be impacted negatively. In addition, the costs of evacuating, treating, relocating, integrating casualties and refugees, and ensuing libel suits would impact regional economies similar to levels of the worst natural disasters. It is also possible that the weapons-using power would suffer investor flight and other negative financial consequences tied to a loss of legitimacy on the world stage..

More than 110 multinationals do business in India's financial capital of Mumbai, including Citigroup, Bank of America, Goldman Sachs, Morgan Stanley and JPMorgan Chase as well as a number of India's financial companies, three largest companies, and Bollywood.[97] The November 2008 terrorist attacks in southern Mumbai not only shook the multinationals but also have Indian government officials worried that Mumbai's protection may be not enough to keep international and domestic businesses located there. The recent attack on Mumbai is minuscule compared to what would result if Mumbai suffered a nuclear-related attack. Such an attack might seem attractive to terrorists, but, as we are now seeing, the world economy is sufficiently interconnected that the waves of financial destruction would likely engulf the aggressor as well.

THE FUTURE

It is becoming harder to argue that nuclear weapons provide unique benefits that justify their enormous downsides. Two other

---

[97] Srivastava, M. & Lakshman, N., "How Risky is India?" *BusinessWeek.* Dec. 4, 2008.
http://www.businessweek.com/magazine/content/08_50/b4112024094731.htm

classes of weapons, biological and chemical, have been outlawed and are being destroyed by their holders.

Four elder American statesmen have proposed that the United States take the initiative to remove some of the immediate nuclear threats like the missiles on alert while negotiating with the other nuclear powers to reduce the numbers of nuclear weapons verifiably.[98] As we write this article in December 2008, a new organization, Global Zero,[99] is being formed, with 100 initial signatories who include former governmental ministers and humanitarian leaders. Simultaneously with its rollout in Paris, David Miliband, the United Kingdom Foreign Secretary, and Nicholas Sarkozy, President of the European Union, published statements[100] reinforcing the goals of Global Zero.

Many years of negotiations would be necessary to bring all nations having nuclear weapons into a treaty banning nuclear weapons. The treaty could provide for an intermediate stage in which no country held more than a few hundred nuclear weapons total. Until now, only deployed nuclear weapons have been limited by treaty. As the numbers decrease, total numbers must be controlled. At present, the United States maintains a "strategic reserve" of undeployed weapons. Although the Moscow Treaty provides for a goal of 1700-2200 deployed nuclear weapons by the

---

[98] George P. Shultz, William J. Perry, Henry A. Kissinger and Sam Nunn, "A World Free of Nuclear Weapons," *The Wall Street Journal,* January 4, 2007; Page A15. http://www.fcnl.org/issues/item.php?item_id=2252&issue_id=54
George P. Shultz, William J. Perry, Henry A. Kissinger and Sam Nunn, "Toward A Nuclear-Free World," *The Wall Street Journal,* January 15, 2008. http://www.nti.org/c_press/TOWARD_A_NUCLEAR_FREE_WORLD_OPED_0115 08.pdf
[99] http://www.globalzero.org/welcome
[100] David Miliband, "A World Without Nuclear Weapons," *The Guardian,* December 8, 2008. http://www.guardian.co.uk/commentisfree/2008/dec/08/nuclear-nuclearpower
The text of the Sarkozy letter to UN Secretary-General Ban Ki-Moon seems not to be available on the Internet. A news article can be found here: http://www.nytimes.com/2008/12/09/world/europe/09france.html

year 2012, the actual numbers held by the United States are likely to be twice to three times that goal.

Verification will provide confidence that the goals are being observed. All weapons materials and the weapons themselves will have to be inventoried by an international body. The IAEA's responsibilities might be increased, or a new body might be formed with similar verification responsibilities for weapons only. This will be a new regime requiring a level of transparency that the states holding nuclear weapons are now resistant to.

The United States and Russia, with inventories of nuclear weapons still in the thousands, will have to lead, but it would be wise to include other states, with and without nuclear weapons, from the beginnings of the negotiations. Non nuclear weapon states will have significant input on the credibility of any process to be developed. Early steps should include taking missiles off alert, ratifying the Comprehensive Nuclear Test-Ban Treaty, and beginning serious negotiations on a treaty ending the manufacture of fissile material for weapons.

Movement toward such a treaty would allow non-state proliferation to be treated as criminal activity and would allow normal criminal justice standards to be applied to cases like that of the Tinners, while providing public confirmation that appropriate punishment is being applied in legal ways.

Moving toward elimination of nuclear weapons is the natural next step after the NPT. The alternative is the hodge-podge of measures toward the non-NPT states that we have seen in the past several years, with continuing uncertainty over how to handle the NPT provision that all states may have civilian fuel cycles. Outlawing of nuclear weapons for all nations, combined with stringent inspection and verification, will make the world a safer place as we move toward the goal.

INTO THE COMPLEX TERRAIN

TIM STEVENS

In 2001 Ayman al-Zawahiri stated that the media war was "an independent battle that we must launch side by side with the military battle."101 This exemplified the importance that al Qaeda attached to their dedicated engagement in international media space. Five years later Secretary Rumsfeld admitted '[o]ur enemies have skillfully adapted to fighting wars in today's media age, but ... our country has not.'102 Since the 1990s global insurgents have used traditional and new media for their own ends. Although counterinsurgency practitioners and theorists are reducing the gap noted by Rumsfeld in their own media practices, use of information technologies continues to constitute a force-multiplier benefiting the insurgents.

However, it is wise not to over-estimate the proficiency of al Qaeda and their affiliates in their use of "new" media, a point made convincingly by Daniel Kimmage early in 2008103. The recent online question-and-answer session between al-Zawahiri and his adherents illustrated the fact that the al Qaeda ideologue neither fully understood the immediacy and expectations of the zero-time global internet, nor relished the ability of Muslims globally to challenge him on the issues concerning them about al Qaeda's motives and operations. In many ways, al Qaeda's media campaign, despite its efficacy relative to their opponents, fails to exploit the potential of the technologies to which they have access. But al Qaeda should not be held up as the exemplar of the future

---

101 Quoted in Jarret M. Brachman (2006), 'High-Tech Terror: al Qaeda's Use of New Technology', *The Fletcher Forum of World Affairs*, Vol.30, No.2, pp.149-164 (http://fletcher.tufts.edu/forum/archives/pdfs/30-2pdfs/brachman.pdf)
102 BBC (2006), 'US 'losing media war to al Qaeda", *BBC Online*, 17 February 2006 (http://news.bbc.co.uk/1/hi/world/americas/4725992.stm)
103 Daniel Kimmage (2008), *The al Qaeda Media Nexus*, RFE-RL Special Report, March 2008 (http://docs.rferl.org/en-US/AQ_Media_Nexus.pdf)

direction of media-savvy insurgents or terrorists. There are myriad other signs that violent actors of many different persuasions might pose security threats in the 21st century, as cyberspace increasingly becomes battlespace.

This essay will not concern itself overly with "cyberwar" or "cyberterrorism." These are important developments in the history of conflict, in which information space is increasingly contested, but they are extensions of ancient tactics of attempting to cripple enemy infrastructure and materiel. Although an electronic "Pearl Harbor," as Deputy Secretary of Defense John Hamre suggested to a congressional hearing in 1998[104], has yet to occur, there is little doubt that critical nodes of information infrastructure remain vulnerable to attack[105], and that cyberattacks can "potentially be a weapon of mass disruption"[106]. The fallout from an attack of this nature is unknown, although information networks tend to be far more resilient than, for example, oil pipelines or transport networks. This inbuilt redundancy was a stated design objective in the development of the military ARPANET in the 1960s, which later developed into today's global internet.

The internet is but one element of cyberspace, which Sam Liles has recently defined as "the terrain of technology-mediated communication"[107]. This broad definition encapsulates not only the hardware that constitutes the internet, and non-internet systems

---

[104] Statement of The Honorable John J. Hamre, Deputy Secretary of Defense, to 1998 Congressional Hearings on Intelligence and Security (http://fas.org/irp/congress/1998_hr/98-06-11hamre.htm)
[105] Georgia Tech Information Security Center (2009), *Emerging Cyber Threats Report for 2009* (http://www.gtisc.gatech.edu/pdf/CyberThreatsReport2009.pdf)
[106] Major-General William Lord, head of provisional USAF Cyber Command, in Bettina H. Chavanne, "USAF Cyber Command Winnows Base List," *Aviation Week*, 17 October 2008.
(http://www.aviationweek.com/aw/generic/story_channel.jsp?channel=defense&id=news/CYBER10178.xml)
[107] Samuel Liles (2008), "Air force cyberspace symposia: Loose ends in cyber space," *Selil Blog*, 21 July 2008 (http://selil.com/?p=239)

like cell phones, satellites, air traffic control, weapons guidance and financial trading networks, but importantly also the people that use this gadgetry in their daily lives. Although we are leaving behind the idea that all computer networks are human networks[108], it remains the case for the time being that people are the most important elements in this cybernetic system. Amongst all the hardware and software, it is the "wetware" of the human mind that remains the most potent factor in any consideration of cyberspace.

However, cyberspace is far larger and more varied than the relatively esoteric motives and actions of the techno-elite. Ordinary people are experiencing more of their lives through cyberspatial media, whether it is email, social networking, file- and media sharing, VOIP telephony, web forums, blogs, or just surfing the web with Google. Many also participate in massive gaming systems like EVE Online, Lineage II and World of Warcraft. Cyberspace extends further into the home with the convergence of digital television, games consoles and broadband. Even the domestic car is situated at the nexus between sensor nets, GPS and entertainment system. How this digital convergence encourages and facilitates different modes of existence and expression is yet to be played out, but we can see the beginnings of these trends in virtual worlds.

Virtual worlds are harbingers of future cyberspace. They combine the interactivity of real life with the freedom of expression and movement denied to many in their physical lives.

A virtual world was recently defined by Mark Bell of Indiana University as "a synchronous, persistent network of people, represented as avatars, facilitated by networked computers." [109] The

---

[108] Barry Wellman (2001), "Computer Networks As Social Network,", *Science*, Vol.293, pp.2031-2034.
[109] Mark W. Bell (2008), "Toward a Definition of " 'Virtual Worlds' ", *Journal of Virtual Worlds Research*, Vol.1, No.1
(https://journals.tdl.org/jvwr/article/view/283/214)

natural world is a complex system of billions of actors, human or otherwise, which interact in multiple ways and with unexpected consequences. Our social world is also a massively tangled web that defies total explanation and prediction, although its components and parameters are broadly amenable to scientific and philosophical consensus. Bell's definition suggests that a virtual world is similarly a multiplex of human activity, endeavor and emotion, with emergent behavior continually surprising the architects of these environments.

This is true of cyberspace more generally, and violence has always emerged in these fast-evolving environments. In the pre-internet days of the early 1980s, white supremacist groups in the US leapt on the new telephone-enabled bulletin boards as a means to propagandize, organize and raise funds. The phenomenon of "griefing" arose in the earliest of networked environments, usually as game-players decided it was more fun to disrupt others' games than to abide by the societal rules that emerged in these spaces.

This should not surprise us. Whether we follow notions of the archetypal trickster, the systems accident of Ernst Bloch or Paul Virilio, or even Murphy's Law, we shouldn't expect things always to proceed as planned. Early internet utopians like Peter Ludlow knew full well that technology contained within itself the seeds of both creation and destruction. The paths of this evolution were never going to be traced in advance, and the internet in particular has proven to be a Darwinian test-bed of false leads, dead-ends, viral contagion, and unexpected successes. The unpredictability and sheer vibrancy of cyberspace has been driven both by its own complexity and by that of the people that interact with it.

Violence fits right in with both the Darwinian metaphor and with human networks. Life online might not be as "nasty, brutish and short" as Thomas Hobbes' natural condition of mankind but there is little doubt that as societies evolve in cyberspace so too do people's abilities to inflict violence upon their neighbors.

"Terrorists use the Internet just like everybody else.", remarked former White House cybersecurity chief Richard Clarke in 2004[110]. Clarke was a deal smarter than many of his contemporaries, and it's no criticism of him that he felt the need to point out the obvious. But, as already noted, with the exception of skilled hackers and cyberwarriors, the world's best known terrorists are lagging in their use of the internet. What is everyone else doing? And why are states becoming more interested in them?

The example of Second Life is illustrative of how people are enacting forms of violence unheard of even in these days of rampant griefing. Whilst they are broadly analogous to traditional real-world activities, the fact they are occurring in a virtual world is giving states pause for thought[111.]

Almost as soon as Second Life was launched in 2003, Linden Research, Inc., the "coding authority" in Edward Castronova's terms[112], was the subject of a revolt against the in-world taxation system. The perpetrators of this "Second Life Boston Tea Party" revolted against the "state" on which they were dependent for their existence, and ultimately forced Linden's hand. A "Declaration of Independence" was duly declared.

In the same year, a full-blown confrontation developed as the "War of Jessie Wall." situated in a "killing zone" in Second Life. For reasons too complex to describe here, this developed from a

---

[110] William New (2004), 'Former cybersecurity chief opposes new regulations', *Government Executive*, 24 May 2004
(http://www.govexec.com/dailyfed/0504/052404tdpm2.htm)
[111] This concept will be examined in more detail in Stevens (forthcoming), "Violence and Virtual Worlds'" Insurgency Research Group.
[112] Edward Castronova (2006), *Synthetic Worlds: The Business and Culture of Online Games*, Chicago: University of Chicago Press, p.151.

disputed land grab into a proxy war over the US invasion of Iraq. A multitude of weapons were deployed, and many avatars were killed (if only for a limited period, of course).

In 2006, anti-racism protestors launched barrages of scripted weapons against an office of Front National Jeunesse, forcing them to move location. In the wake of the 2004 Madrid train bombings arson attacks were mutually launched against in-world offices of the two main Spanish political parties, in protest at the Zapatista government's decision to negotiate with ETA.

These protests, and many other examples, were all political in nature and most had real world analogues. Interestingly though, the first of these was truly existential in nature, and this trend has developed further with movements like the Second Life Liberation Army—"the establishment of basic political 'rights' for avatars"— who have succeeded in damaging in-world stores owned by multinationals like Reebok and American Apparel.[113]

That people are protesting tax or rights is a sure sign that social and political structures are developing strongly in virtual worlds. This is again no surprise to both advocates and critics of cyberspace. These alternative governance and organizational structures are likely to evolve further, and may begin to challenge traditional political structures outside cyberspace.

But these scenarios are secondary to the general convergence of the real and the virtual. With embedded sensor networks, ubiquitous urban computing, and augmented reality, it may become increasingly difficult to "tell the difference" between the

---

[113] The Second Life Liberation Army has since been revealed to have been an experiment carried out by an anonymous security professional. The events carried out by the SLLA remain relevant as they illustrate the capabilities actual hostile actors could carry out in virtual worlds and the public and commercial reactions to such actions.

two. Indeed, as urban governance degrades and cities effectively become feral, information may become the glue that holds societies together[114]. In another sense, they already do in rural areas dependent upon cell phones for social and economic cohesion.

Richard J. Norton, who first floated the "feral city" hypothesis, envisaged urban areas where state influence has effectively disappeared, to be replaced by the bottom-up rule of violence. These cities would maintain commercial links with the outside world, either through licit or illicit channels, and would exert "an almost magnetic influence on terrorist organizations."[115]

The denizens of such places would have access to information technologies, further connecting them with the international system. This would enable them to reorganize in cyberspace, forming new networks of support, influence and economy. These virtual governance structures will be a substantial challenge to even those states whose cities have yet to "go feral." Cyberspace is inherently transnational, despite fears of the balkanization of the internet, and the searching tendrils emanating from a fractured city will not only not respect national borders, but will not even recognize their existence.

The phenomenon of global jihadism already displays some of these characteristics, and global media space rivals physical space as the critical battlefield for the global insurgent. As people live greater parts of their lives mediated through cyberspace, this will itself become a contested landscape.

---

[114] Tim Stevens (2008), "Information Landscapes and the Feral City," *Ubiwar*, 24 September 2008 (http://ubiwar.com/2008/09/24/information-landscapes-and-the-feral-city/)
[115] Richard J. Norton (2003), "Feral Cities: The New Strategic Environment," *Naval War College Review*, Autumn 2003, pp.97-106.
(http://findarticles.com/p/articles/mi_moJIW/is_4_56/ai_110458726)

States are trying hard to "horizon-scan" in their strategic planning, with initiatives exploring virtual worlds, cyberwar and autonomous agents, but it is hard to see how any can prepare fully for a world in which information, of which we are all constructed, becomes pure battlespace. New formulations and doctrine will be required to undertake counterinsurgency and counterterrorism operations in theatres for which the rules are very much unwritten. This is particularly true of environments where human behavior might appear similar to that of the real world but in which intervention might produce highly variable and counter-productive side-effects.

The greatest worry for states must surely be that as they rely heavily on cyberspace already for their command and control structures, they cannot simply flip the switch on troublesome cyberspace communities. In the case of the feral city, kinetic intervention may remain the only solution but once bitten in Mogadishu, twice shy perhaps.

The intervention logic might not be readily apparent but as more companies invest in, and take profits from, virtual spaces like Second Life and Habbo, states may decide to protect wealth-generating businesses. They would certainly do so if their own assets are jeopardized in these environments or if parallel political structures threaten their pre-eminence and monopoly on violence. We have seen the results of the declaration of war on a tactic; what might a similar campaign look like in cyberspace when waged against a whole mode of existence?

Virtual worlds provide signs that social structures and human concerns are expressing themselves through violent acts strongly correspondent with terrorism and insurgency, whilst infant cyberwar is a battle for critical infrastructure and influence. The convergence of these phenomena, and others yet to emerge, will play out in the navigable and complex terrain of cyberspace.

SIMULATED "BLACK SWANS": NATIONAL SECURITY, PERCEPTION OPERATIONS, AND THE EXPANSION OF THE INFOSPHERE

ADAM ELKUS

The rapid expansion of the infosphere poses major challenges for traditional modes of national security analysis, operational art, and intelligence production. Part of our problem with the future comes from the clash between our expectations and reality, as the information metaspace of the 21st century is not the utopian community space predicted by the great futurists of the 20th. We are not living in Marshall McLuhan's harmonious "Global Village"; we now inhabit the cacophonous silicon slums depicted in the cyberpunk novels of William Gibson and his numerous imitators. A biblical flood of information has confused rather than clarified, deconstructing meanings, dualities, and constructs we once took for granted. The frighteningly realistic reproduction of the real seen on our TV sets and increasingly our video game screens blurs the line between mimesis and simulacra. And complexity gives rise to emergent phenomena that complicate traditional methods of explanation and prediction—we look on the horizons to see a world of Black Swans.

It is within this ruined landscape that the insurgent wages an omnidirectional war of perception against hierarchal organizations that still believe in the teleological certainties of a world of mechanistic systems. In an evolutionary step from Mao, the revolutionary swims in a sea of information, disguising himself within the digital exaflood that has come to characterize modern life. To fight the modern terrorist and insurgent, our analysis and doctrine must also evolve to meet the conditions of a fundamentally chaotic age.

The crisis presented by the rapidly shifting information landscape is also an opportunity for counterinsurgents and counter-terrorists to become truly "super-empowered." In order to do so, we must first recognize the tremendous changes wrought by the evolution of the infosphere, and their effects on both operational doctrine and analysis.

GLOBAL BRAIN VS. SIMULACRA

Since the enlightenment, some philosophers and scientists have seen human history as a teleological evolution towards human omniscience. In this view, with each new scientific discovery, we march closer to a communion with God. In the 20th century, philosophers for the first time were able to conceive of a global emergent intelligence able to encompass the whole of human knowledge. Science fiction author H.G. Wells predicted a permanent encyclopedia that encompassed the whole of human memory and knowledge, available to all. Such a massive store of knowledge would foreshadow a massive "intellectual unification." Wells' idea sounds eerily like Wikipedia, a borderless information commons maintained by a transnational array of volunteers.

The Catholic philosopher Teilhard De Chardin popularized the notion of the noosphere, a global conscious network that encompassed the totality of human thought and interaction. As the complexity of human social networks grows, this distributed consciousness will eventually reach self-awareness. The media theorist Marshall McLuhan also shared this idea of a global information commons acting as a kind of biological nerve system— after all, his book *Understanding Media* is subtitled *The Extensions of Man*. Finally, there is the "nerd rapture" of the Singularity— electronics gurus Vernor Vinge and Ray Kurzweil's idea of the moment when man and self-aware machines achieve a kind of superhuman intelligence that will free humanity from the constraints of its origins. Needless to say, these theories are based on the presumption that history marches forward—that every new advance brings us closer to a desired end state. The French postmodernist philosopher Jean Baudrillard had a more cynical view. "We believe naively that the progress of Good, its advance in all fields (the sciences, technology, democracy, human rights) corresponds to a defeat of evil," Baudrillard wrote in *The Spirit of Terrorism*. "Good and Evil advance together, as part of the same movement. ...[Good] does not conquer evil, nor indeed does the reverse happen; they are at once irreducible to each other and inextricably interrelated."

Instead of a world of collective information and human knowledge, Baudrillard predicted a future dystopia dominated by copies without originators—the simulacra. Simulacra is not the illusory virtual world that is depicted in The Matrix, the movie that introduced most Americans to his philosophy (although Baudrillard claimed it was a distortion of it). Instead, simulacra is a simulation of something that never existed in the first place. Simulacra is a mixture of signs with no real world reference—they only point back to themselves. The classic example of this "hyperreal" phenomena in Baudrillard's work is Disneyland. It is a monument to fantasy, populated by cartoon characters who mingle among a landscape taken out of Disney products. Yet if you kick one of the many Mickey Mouses wandering around you'll be hurting an underpaid college student. The Potemkin village of Disneyland is more real than real.

Baudrillard's most provocative argument is that the world has become Disneyland. The expanding virtual reality generated by the roaring global consumer machine and the expansion of technology is quickly outstripping what we know of reality, creating a world of pseudo-events. Needless to say, this denial of reality is an extreme view, leading to nihilism if taken literally. In Baudrillard's world, Brian Massumi notes, human beings float as "satellites in aimless orbit around an empty center," existing within a world without meaning. Baudrillard himself jumped the shark with his famous statement that the Gulf War didn't take place, something that came as news to the many soldiers who had fought in it.

One might say that the techno-utopians have been vindicated. The noosphere has been realized in the virtual layer created by 24-hour television networks, mobile electronics, and the expansive metasphere of the Internet. Wells' idea of a permanent encyclopedia has also been achieved in the form of the World Wide Web's free-floating mass of information. Anyone can use a free Blogspot or Wordpress blog to express their personal identity or political opinions, while communities work together through wikis and open-source. Virtual worlds allow individuals to escape from their ordinary lives and become all-powerful sorcerers or plasma-rifle wielding alien hunters, alone or with friends. As cloud computing shifts computing functions online, the colonization of the information frontier shows no signs of stopping anytime soon.

PERCEPTION, ONTOLOGY, AND ANARCHY

Baudrillard's apocalyptic view of the future, however, is an inevitable byproduct of technological progress. For all of the wonder of the Internet, huge amounts of the digital ether are taken up by porn, conspiracy theories, and automated spam and advertisements constructed by roving bots. This ever-expanding digital landfill forms a kind of shadow Internet symbiotic to the "real" metasphere championed by Silicon Valley hype men. Sadly, digital spam mirrors the increasing onslaught of offline junk information we are bombarded with every day. The onslaught of contextless television imagery Neil Postman warned of in *Amusing Us To Death* seems remarkably quaint in this era of massive "reality" TV spectacles, faked political scandals, and conspiracy theories enabled through modern media—to say nothing of the avalanche of unwanted advertisements, hoaxes, and ideological appeals we encounter on a day to day basis.

Baudrillard's simulacra is also visible in the massive virtual worlds that the power of the infosphere has made viable. Laugh all you want at your coworker with a level 110 Elf Ranger, but he is participating in an alternate social ecosystem of remarkable complexity. Second Life and World of Warcraft are virtual colonies in the most traditional sense—promised lands for those wanting to make bank. They have thriving economies based around the exchange of goods and property, even if those goods don't really "exist" in the most literal sense of the term. Second Life and World of Warcraft magnates make a decent living off of non-existent goods in a fantasy world populated by Orcs and Elves, putting the lie to your mother's constant admonitions that playing video games will never get you anywhere in life.

The merge of the virtual and the real that science fiction authors have predicted since the eighties is occurring at a rapid rate. Real-life personalities make appearances in Second Life and organizations ranging from the United Nations and the Army have set up digital outposts. Baudrillard also wouldn't be surprised with the massive Synthetic Environment for Analysis and Simulations (SEAS), a giant simulator constructed by the Defense Department to massively mirror real-world people and events. He might have seen it as the real-life visualization of Jorge Luis Borges' map of the empire—a map that shifted in real time to match the empire's fortunes.

The merger of the virtual and the real also multiplies identity's fluidity. Old dualities break down under the weight of technology and an aggressively hybridizing popular culture. Globalization itself is aggressively modifying identities and aggressively challenging traditional identities and cultures. New identities such as the dizzying array of youth subcultures and neo-traditional primordialists such as the global Islamist sphere coexist uneasily and even cross-pollinate. Old concepts of patriotism and sovereignty are being eroded as global networks of law, commerce, and culture dissect the traditional state.

One consequence of this fluidity of identity is a phenomenon sociologist Zygmunt Bauman calls "liquid life." In liquid life, one is always striving to avoid being left behind, and the vehicle for doing so is frenetic self-marketing. The explosion of blogging and social media has turned the exposition of the self into an art form. In order to get friends, jobs, and romantic partners, we must cram the totality of our being into a small profile page on a social networking site. One might consider school shooters as extreme examples of viral marketers in their violent attempts to draw the attention of the world. From this perspective, there is precious little that separates the elaborate hoax of Lonelygirl15 from the narcissistic rampage of Virginia Tech mass murderer Seung-Hui Cho.

Identity's flux finds its parallel in the fragmentation of the news media. Classical journalism was once a unitary provider of meaning to the public; world-defining public events such as the Kennedy assassination and the moon landing were communal experiences realized through a handful of media outlets. With the social media evolution, users increasingly customize their news consumption as a lifestyle choice, piecing together bits and pieces of news from a dizzying array of sources. The financial decline of the newspaper industry may lead to a hyper-localism, with an open-source array of bloggers crowd-sourcing news coverage in their communities. A preview of this can be seen in the reaction to the Mumbai attacks, where the most accurate information was assembled through blogs, Twitter, and social networking profiles.

But in a world where anyone can produce news, the boundary between true and false—always ephemeral—grows ever more tenuous. We have always had propaganda, but viral propaganda can boomerang around the infosphere unchallenged by slow-moving hierarchal organizations. By the time false information is challenged, it will have already made its mark. Although Richard Dawkins' idea of the meme—a self-replicating cultural organism that competes with other ideas in a Darwinian struggle for survival—is flawed, there is truth in the notion that ideas do have lives of their own. In fact, future historians may conclude that urban legends and conspiracies were the first real religion of the modern age—our version of Zeus, Zoroaster, and Athena.

We are witnessing a convergence of conspiracy theories, alternate religions, racial myths, and alien sightings that form what fringe culture researcher Michael Barkun calls the "conspiratorial milieu"—an emerging unified conspiracy theory that relates every single alien, Bigfoot sighting, and JFK "grassy knoll" shooter together. In fact, political science professor Jodi Dean sees conspiracy theories as a kind of radical populism that has gone unnoticed by the powers that be, seeking to challenge the establishment's control over discourse with forms of counter-knowledge. If so, it goes to prove Baudrillard's point that these populists can only challenge the establishment using the language of popular culture, as the aesthetics of the 9/11 conspiracy video "Loose Change" mirrored that of the popular television series The X-Files.

Warfare in the age of simulacra means a switch from information operations to perception warfare. What is being contested is not the truth, but the means by which we judge it. The enemy is waging perception operations against us, hijacking our very ability to perceive reality.

PERCEPTION OPERATIONS AND VIRAL VIDEO INSURGENCY

Insurgents and terrorists cloak themselves within the noise of the infosphere, utilizing conspiracy theories, rumor, propaganda, and deception as the equivalent of ground cover that an infantryman uses to hide from machine-gun fire. Terrorists, criminal-insurgents, and other non-state forces mass their forces in cyberspace, as military theorist Robert Bunker notes, only to suddenly coalesce in a swarming attack and then disappear. Some theorists in the emerging field of "Fifth Generation Warfare" also see a puppet-master potential in the ability of a single manipulator or emergent groupings of manipulators to pull the strings of a mass of unwitting or compartmentalized pawns. Such a hidden force would use the white noise of contradictory information as a means of concealing their own involvement, engineering a situation without their opponents ever realizing their presence.

Emergent organizations formed in the heat of the moment or organized as pawns for in a "plug and play" move for a terrorist group could also create a maze of copycats that will confuse the analyst by increasing the bottom end of the signal-to-noise ratio. The analyst will search in vain for an originator, a mastermind, a puppet-master, to find nothing. Several examples of this tactic can be found in Iraq. Abu Abdullah al-Rashid al-Baghdadi, the leader of the Islamic State of Iraq was exposed by the US military as a fake created by al Qaeda to put an Iraqi face on the organization. Adding to the confusion were reports by the Iraqi government that Baghdadi had been killed and a similar claim by Al-Arabiya TV that Baghdadi was a former Iraqi Army officer turned insurgent. There is also the case of the Youtube sniper Juba, an insurgent sniper whose videotaped operations frightened combat personnel and motivated insurgent sympathizers. It is hard to tell whether Juba is one person, several, a fiction created to lower morale, or an emergent phenomenon that encompasses all of these possibilities at the same time.

The fluidity of identity provides a means of cover and advantage for the insurgent. The insurgent already has mastered the dimensional switch from civilian to combatant, but evidence of insurgent exploitation of virtual worlds shows insurgents switching from real to virtual in order to provide a means of training and communication beyond the prying eyes of spy agencies. Identity can also be shifted, as the insurgent becomes a chameleon to please all. al Qaeda's propaganda masters attempt to play the role of both political leaders and theologians, elucidating concern for any and all Islamic cause—al Qaeda is at once Palestinian, Chechen, Saudi, Egyptian, and Indonesian.

Identity gives rise to a related question—how do we attribute responsibility for attacks in a world characterized by fractured networks of dummy fronts, murky criminal groups, splinter cells, and state-sponsored cyber militias? The problem of attribution becomes particularly pressing in the world of cyber-insurgency, where an electronic trail traced back to a certain point could be simply a hijacked server, or the start point of an automated network of botnets.

Even more difficult than attributing responsibility may be determining the attack's true target. Attacks become multiple information operation loops designed to achieve cascading—and contradictory effects on audiences. Was Mumbai an assault aimed at the Indian state? The West? Pakistan? The Israelis? Terrorist and insurgent operations are increasingly characterized by complex, multi-target omnidirectional forms of information operations able to hit on tactical, operational, and strategic levels simultaneously with little cost to the perpetrator.

Overly mechanistic concepts of operational doctrine have made counter-terrorism and counter-insurgency substantially more difficult. Network-Centric Warfare and Effects-Based-Operations are attempts to try to impose order onto this rapidly chaotic world by conceptualizing it as a machine system that can be manipulated through inputs and outputs. Destroy and target certain linkages through airpower and you can disable the system's "nodes." Applied to counter-terrorism thought, this results in a crude form of reductionism in which network nodes of a cell are taken out, collapsing the organization. If we see the enemy as a system, we can compel its actions through modeling. Destroy X and you will compel Y.

The hubris inherent in network forms of warfare is the presumption that all variables can be computed, and that we can control the human system just as surely as we control the mechanical. As Paul Van Riper noted in his critique of EBO in *Joint Force Quarterly*, human systems are far more dynamic, unpredictable, and adaptive systems than most believe. Attempt to crudely manipulate them and the system will give you a result you do not quite anticipate. In a world where insurgents are increasingly cloaked behind the wall of information, our efforts will most likely result in punching thin air. Even counterinsurgency shares similar conceptual weaknesses. The Maoist era-doctrine of David Galula and Robert Thompson is based on the image of the enemy as a unified, hierarchal cybernetic actor, and the surrounding society as a social organism that the counterinsurgent controls through population-centric counterinsurgency and information operations.

But how do we fight a fragmented enemy that hides in the web of information, composed of emergent groups that manipulate perception? How does one control, predict, or calculate its actions? Ultimately, what Frank G. Hoffman calls "neo-classical counterinsurgency" suffers from the same kind of systems thinking problems of EBO and network-centric warfare—dealing with increasing complexity in complex adaptive human systems.

THE "BLACK SWAN" AND THE ART OF THE ANTI-EXPLANATION

Perhaps our greatest weakness is our insistence on linear explanation, a pox on both our predictions of future operational and strategic conditions and our means of culling the past for questions to current problems. A more complex world of information, mass media, fluid identity, and emergent self-organizing structures is also a much more random one. While philosophy has largely abandoned the linear teleology of Hegel, we still cling to the everyday linear and logical linkage of cause and effect because it is the only reality we know. We explain things in narratives that rationalize what is chaotic, imposing form upon void to justify our actions and make sense of strange phenomena. Unfortunately, such behavior doesn't serve us well when we face disaster.

With every disaster comes the inevitable orgy of finger pointing over who "lost" a certain country or failed to see "the warning signs." But were those signs really so clear? Or, more importantly, was the disruptive event really inevitable? This pre-supposes that disruptive events have linear causes, explanations, and were eminently predictable from the start. Many of these assumptions are false.

Charles Kurzman's book *The Unthinkable Revolution in Iran* rigorously examines each explanation offered for the revolt that launched the revolution and finds each of them lacking. In times of tumult, human actions decisively deviate from otherwise constant social, political, and cultural models. Structures that often provide excellent indicators of behavior break down, and new realities are created. Instead of looking at social science to provide linear, comprehensive explanations, we may be better off searching for anti-explanations.

What Kurzman calls "anti-explanation" eschews retroactive rationalization in favor of "recognizing and reconstructing the lived experience of the moment." Anti-explanation foregrounds the anomalies in the background of linear explanation; it recognizes the power of confusion, the instability of the moment, and the disruption of routine in disruptive events. When we analyze revolution, we often forget that social structures do not persist through inertia, as even stasis takes work to maintain. The old often persists because it gives itself an air of self-fulfilling inevitability, as people will not commit to courses of actions they believe will fail.

But in moments of great change, people rapidly assess and reassess their behavior based on the fragmentary information available to them and the actions of others. This emergent process of assessing the often-ephemeral viability of change produces a kind of viral action that can change the course of history. If a dictator who seemed stable a week ago is overthrown, there is no contradiction in noting that the prior analysis of his strength wasn't entirely incorrect.

As Nicholas Nassim Taleb argues in *The Black Swan,* some events also are so unlikely that their very randomness removes all obstacles to their occurrence. Taleb argues that we are moving towards a more random world where "black swans" may become the norm rather than the exception. People often construct post-hoc rationalizations for these occurrences or claim to have "seen the signs." But there is a small chance that even the most unlikely event could occur, and if it does there will surely be someone out claiming that an institution ignored evidence of its occurrence. Such an action, merely by being willed into existence, becomes more likely in the future and seems retroactively plausible.

On the other hand, some "Black Swans" may also be one-time events. 9/11, for example, had the TSA searching grannies for knives. But the next terrorist, Richard Reid, tried to ignite explosives attached to his shoe. After that, TSA checked shoes. When terrorists tried to use liquid explosives TSA banned all fluids. Targets may remain the same but methods of attack will continuously shift to get around security. Such a process will eventually continue until no carry-ons are allowed on the plane at all.

Either way, the "Black Swan" plays havoc with our logic. Red-team scenarios can alleviate the burden, but how can we plan for every conceivable scenario? Or, to take a different tack, should we? Being strong everywhere means being weak everywhere. One can easily drain organizational resources planning for "movie-plot" terrorism only to be surprised by a group of men with machine guns. The frightening reality of the "Black Swan" is the limit of our prediction and the inadequacy of our explanation. But as Camus' conception of Sisyphus illustrates, just because a goal may be ultimately unattainable does not mean edging closer to it has no social worth. Protecting the national interest is task that must be accomplished regardless of human weakness.

FORCE STRUCTURE FOR PERCEPTION WARFARE

In the last decade, defense reformers have drawn up plans for operational design that meets the challenge of a complex warfare. Among the most elaborate (and interesting) of the new doctrines is Systemic Operational Design (SOD) an Israeli form of operational art created by the Operational Theory Research Institute (OTRI)'s warfare guru Brigadier Gen (ret) Shimon Naveh. SOD avoids the pitfalls of EBO by aiming not to control a looming, chaotic system, but learn about it through the constant injection of operational stimuli. The SOD practitioner observes how it learns and hedges against emergent properties as they emerge. A related concept is Los Angeles Terror Early Warning Group (TEW) analysis, which relies on a multidisciplinary cell that carry out transactional analysis, constantly sorting and re-sorting information from sensors. The operational space is continuously re-evaluated as analysts search for a terrorist "kill chain."

We can also fight the enemy's emergent networks with our own. It's telling that the most exemplary counter-hacker investigation, the Grey Goose project, was a non-governmental effort headed by a diverse array of contributors. Hackers, intel insiders, contractors, and analysts united to discover the true source of Russian cyber-attacks during the Georgian conflict under the direction of former Coast Guard intelligence analyst Jeffrey Carr. An army of these open-source networks can function as Wild West posses operating on a digital frontier. Former Defense Intelligence Agency officer Michael Tanji's has a similar idea that he dubs "Think Tank 2.0." The Think Tank 2.0 approach unites an eclectic array of geographically separated experts hold digital salons on respective topics. Both Grey Goose and Think Tank 2.0 point the way to a future of collapsible organizations task-organized to deal with complex emergencies or produce out-of-the-box analysis.

Networking isn't enough to improve our national security analysis. We also must change the way we think about the future itself. Futurism should not be thought of a scientific enterprise but as a wild carnival of differing narratives, ideas, and perspectives. Futurists are not scientists who are coldly and neutrally looking at the results of experimental data. The future is not a fixed state that can be divined through an astronomer's telescope. Rather, it is the sum of a chaotic mixture of social forces, ideas, and the actions of those determined to change it. The future changes from day to day, and any attempt to predict its outline from supposedly objective criteria is doomed to failure. Many—if not all—radical predictions are ultimately narratives projected through political and cultural prisms.

When we think about the future we are telling ourselves stories, and perhaps we should balance the objectivity of the policymaker with the playfulness of the storyteller. We can use the differing narratives of the future as intellectual frames that we can swap, switch, and fuse as need be to constantly revise our perceptions based on the flux of events and fortunes. If reporting is the first draft of history, prediction is the first draft of the future. But like any other draft, it must be endlessly revised.

Above all, we must remember that our war is not just a struggle against a cunning enemy but our own human flaws. These flaws have been magnified by technology. But with grit, patience, and innovation we can blog, Twitter, and AIM our way to a more secure America.

AN OUTBREAK OF DEMOCRACY

DANIEL H. ABBOTT

On November 4, 2008, the American people had a choice. Given the choice between change and continuity, the American people rejected change, and selected President Barack Obama.

Barack Obama enters office with little experience for the way things are done. Out of necessity he needs to become an "Establishment President," relying on party leaders and beltway insiders to help him run his government. Unlike John McCain, Barack Obama is ignorant of a great deal of the knowledge that would allow him to act in a radical or novel way.

John McCain knew enough about European politics that if he had wanted to radically change our foreign policy there, he could have. He knew about China, India, and South America that he could make and enforce radical departures from the way things were done. That would have been a risker future, and America is now on a less eventful course.

The greatest threat in the age of Obama will not come from Vladimir Putin—that António Salazar with nukes—or China, or Hugo Chavez, or even Iran. The greatest threat Obama might face would be a collapse of the Military-Industrial Complex, which he (and we) would not even see coming.

The greatest threat would manifest itself through a sudden outbreak of democracy that would end our secret war, or 5GW, to shrink the Gap.

OF GLOBALIZATION AND PEACE

No understanding of the global environment is complete without awareness to the "Core/Gap" model of the world, developed by Thomas P.M. Barnett in three books: *The Pentagon's*

New Map, Blueprint for Action, and *Great Powers.* Barnett's model is essentially Immanuel Wallerstein's "World Systems" model with a capitalist bent, agreeing with the Marxist geographer that the world is organized into a Core of productive wealth, a "periphery" or "non-integrated gap" of poverty and isolation," and a "Seam" or "Semi-Periphery" seeking admittance into the Core but at risk of a general collapse. Barnett adds to this understanding an emphasis on the power of global trade and finance, along with nuclear weapons, to end wars between powers. Likewise, Barnett emphasis's the beneficial aspects of trade, and advocates that the American government to expand the Core to encompass the entire world.

Not all of Barnett's specific predictions have held up. American forces significantly scaled back their presence" in Central Asia during the Bush Administration, for instance, and Russia has proven to be a country "in the Gap" as it has faced mounting problems over the past twenty years. Still, Barnett's central truth is that American security depends heavily on shrinking the Gap, expanding the Core, and ended war as we have known it. There will always be conflicts and trouble, but with wise leadership we can maintain our leadership position in the world while never again fighting a war with any great power (Britain, China, France Germany, India, Japan, etc.)

We want to expand the Core, shrink the Gap. That will be done by adding countries that are currently in the Seam to the Core, and moving some countries from the Gap to the Seam. The precise definition of what countries are in which category changes over time with circumstances. To illustrate, take this map modified from Wikipedia, with the Core as light gray, the Seam as medium gray, and the Gap as the darkest color:

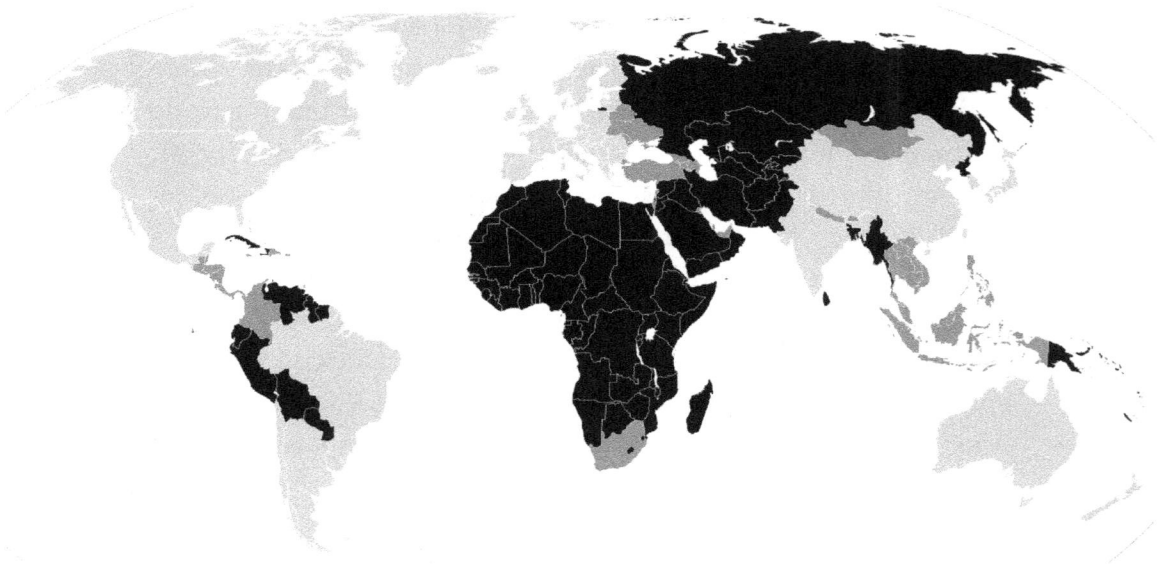

Figure 1. Core, Seam and Gap. (Illustration by Dan Abbott)

Absorbing the Seam of course means opening up trade, capital flows, and immigration, but it also means more than that too. It means processing a fighting force that can keep the Seam safe from Gap predators and a stabilization force capable of helping those countries recover from disasters. For instance, the clear interest of NATO in the Baltic States of Lithuania, Latvia, and Estonia has doubtless allowed those countries to worry about things others than Russian tanks. Likewise, while Georgia did not possess the security guarantees of the Baltic States, the world's rapid reaction to Russia's invasion during the Olympic Games have allowed that country to begin rebuilding, providing housing for refugees and infrastructure to provide jobs.

Life in the Gap is nasty, brutish, and short. Gap states export violence, host disease, and force wealth-creating countries to divert attention from creating wealth (if they are in the Core) or joining the Core (if they are in the Seam). Shrinking the gap is the greatest challenge of the 21st century—both in the Age of Obama and beyond. Presuming there is not a catastrophic breakdown of the global system, no one can stop this, except the people.

OF CONFLICTS AND WARS

Wars are categorized into several "gradients" or "generations" based on the conflict's concentration of violence. Considering these gradients in the context of cognition (where the first stage of observing the world, the last is acting on the world, , we can say that the most concentrated violence is aimed at preventing an enemy from being able to act in any way, by killing him, while the most dispersed violence is aimed at preventing the enemy from observing that there is a war to fight, thus sparing him. While the interplay of cognition and violence is outlined at length the books *The John Boyd Roundtable* and *Revolutionary Strategies in Early Christianity,* a visual depiction of these gradients contrasted against the cognitive cycle is as follows:

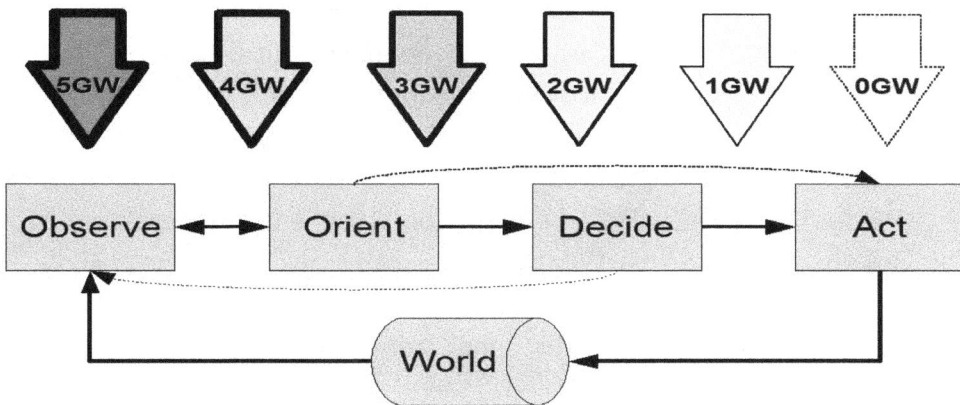

Figure 2. The OODA loop.

Conflicts among the people are of two types: 4GW and 5GW. In both of these, the difference between civilians and combatants becomes academic. A 4GW can be so peaceful that the enemy warfighter may be misclassified as a criminal, a bandit, or even a loon. Warfighters disperse into the population, and explain special legal protections given to civilians to their advantage. America's highest-profile defeat, Vietnam, was a 4GW where the enemy sapped our will to fight and changed our orientation to turn us against our client, the Republic of Vietnam. However, while a 4GW seeks to change the enemy's will and orientation, a 5GW seeks to blind the enemy to one's existence by manipulating pawns who appear to be the real players.

5GW can be subcategorized into three main types: Insurgent 5GW, State-Exporting 5GW, and State-Automating 5GW. First, Insurgent 5GW, is the classical formulation where a small cell attempts to influence political conflicts in such a way that its own goals are achieved, without the people realizing it. In American history, the Anti-Masonic Party (1828-1838) believed that it was combating an Insurgent 5GW in which an insurgent 5GW manipulated the actions of the State. The Anti-Masons believed that the prominent political parties at the time were both being manipulated by the Masons. Second, State-Exporting 5GWs are where a sovereign state engages in similar methods to achieve similar goals. The anti-Catholic nativist movement (1845-1860), for instance, believed that it was combating a State-Exporting 5GW organized by the Vatican. The anti-Catholics believed that the political players of the time were stooges for the Pope. Third, A State-Automating 5GW, an example of which is the centerpiece of this chapter, is a Secret War by a state against itself with the goal of permanently operating the machinery of the state in a way that cannot be undone by subsequent administrations without the awareness of the people.

The most prominent example of a State-Automating 5GW is the Military-Industrial-Complex that helped us win the cold war. It is still needed, but the only reason it is needed is that the people cannot be trusted.

OF THE PEOPLE AND THEIR WEAKNESS

America cannot win a 4GW—a long-term war of ideas—because the American people will betray her first. Within a generation of the enslavement of Europe and China to Stalinism, arrogant American liberals combined with comfortable American leftists to do their best to defeat American action in the Vietnam War, and make South-East Asia safe for Communism. If history repeats itself, or at least rhymes, within a generation of 9/11 active support of al Qaeda inspired movements should be fashionable on college campuses.

The reason that this treasonous behavior is more common among the left and the right is pretty clear: a long-standing political tradition in the United States is the rejection of powerful voices as bad because they are powerful. Academic Marxists and 'Critical theorists' use terms such as oppression, hegemonism, and such to describe this phenomenon, while populists criticize the "Eastern Establishment" and elites, but the consistent suspicion of what we have because we have it is clear. Further, once any dispute becomes part of public consciousness, it tends to be debased into the typical Democratic v. Republican dispute, which means eventually which party is against the consensus on a particular will take power and kill the effort.

As a method of defending our country, 4GW is bankrupt. The struggle for minds, if we try to use methods of public diplomacy, branding, and so on, is a strategy destined for defeat. The people will not tolerate a sustained effort to achieve any grand unifying objective. They do not have the trust or the willpower required for such a crusade.

While America cannot win a 4GW, she can win a 5GW—a war of hidden movements. America won the Cold War because, in spite of losing popular support for the struggle against Communism, she created institutions that kept the war going regardless of the will of the people—even regardless of the will of the United States

Congress, which cut aid to allies such as the Republic of Vietnam and the Khmer Republic.. It was the Military-Industrial-Complex that gave America the ability to win.

To triumph in this protracted struggle to spread globalization, America must fight a 5GW to protect the effort from the changing whims of the people. The State-Automating 5GW that was originally created to defeat Communism is morphing into a win this Long War against al Qaeda and her friends, we have to fight a 5GW. Our method of fighting is our Military-Industrial-Complex, transformed to shrink the gap. Secretary of Defense Robert Gates, who served under President Bush and now serves under President Obama, is but one figure in this transformation. Because of this State-Automating 5GW, an iron triangle of bureaucrats, contractors, and Congressmen will support our struggle out of reasons that have nothing to do with ideology. While the people are weak, the system is strong.

OF THE SYSTEM AND ITS STRENGTH

America currently subverts her own population in her effort to spread globalization. This is because making shrinking the Gap is a public policy option means that the public could reject the option.. Shrinking the Gap is a long-term process, and should be insulated from politics as much as possible. The anti-Communist 5GW that was built up at the beginning of the Cold War is still functioning in spite of widespread recognition that is has been obsoleted by its own success. That same structure is becoming a Gap-integrating machine, a State-Automating 5GW that locks our country into possessing the strength necessary to make globalization more durable. Republicans and Democrats, liberals and conservatives, globalists and internationalists, they come-and-go. Their electoral defeats and victories are as rational as which town is hit by which tornado, which Senator uses an anti-Asian slur that was current among North African Jews a lifetime ago, and other quirks of fate. Shrinking the Gap is too important to be left to chance.

The Military-Industrial-Complex has existed since the National Security Act of 1947. It includes the Congress, including the 435 Representatives and 100 Senators. Likewise, it encompasses the Department of Defense's professional service, both the civilian bureaucracy and the military officer corps. Likewise, the Complex is comprised of all contractors and sub-contractors, from Lockheed-Martin to Boeing to Halliburton. This iron triangle is self-sustaining, because the Congress needs the military to provide jobs to constituents, the military needs to the Congress to provide funds to hire workers and build system, while the voters require Congress to allocate funds to employ them. There is an old saying that there are no atheists in foxholes; whether that is true or not, there are no doves on the Appropriations Committee.

In shrinking the gap, as in most of politics, principles are fine, but steady cash flows are better.

The Military-Industrial-Complex built by the Cold War plays an important role in shrinking the Gap. Many states in the seam or semi-periphery are too poor to both invest in economic growth and defend themselves. Russia's recent invasion of Georgia, for instance, not only destroyed millions of dollars worth of international investment, but also will force countries like Ukraine, Azerbaijan, Kazakhstan, and Moldova to use money building in-depth defense networks that could have otherwise been spent on needed reforms.

The Military-Industrial-Complex is more than a network of weapons systems and bases. It is an impressive structure that undermines democracy in America, constrains policy decisions, and protects us from the whim of the people.

The greatest threat to the United States in the twentieth-century is an outbreak of democracy. We have nothing worse to fear than a collapse of our State-Automating 5GW.

The Military-Industrial-Complex has proven remarkably resilient. It survived the collapse of the Vietnam War, and indeed the collapse of the Cold War. It survived times of recession (where other urgent priorities for the money also demanded attention) and times of peace (when attention moves away from defense generally).

However, a large enough crisis could destroy this equilibrium weakening the iron triangle of Congress, contractors, and voters that the Military-Industrial-Complex is based on, and force our military to seek funding on the same basis as many other agencies. As the American people have a bias toward the short-term and to parochial needs, this would lead to the same underinvestment in shrinking the Gap as we see in education, mass transportation, and other fields.

At present, the best candidate for such a crisis would be the economic and financial collapse of 2008 and 2009. The iron triangle is self-sustaining, but if cries for universal health or industry bailouts, for instance, become loud enough, those Representative and Senators who now protect their seats by funding the Military-Industrial-Complex may get more political mileage out of taking care of sick people and saving industrial jobs.

A military so weakened would not be able to offer security guarantees to countries bordering Russia, secure the peace, help in post-conflict/post-disaster stabilization operations, or be a force for good in the world. We would be left with a larger version of Britain's military, a shadow of our former strength unable to play the role of globalization's fist. The priorities of every country in the world would shrink, as there would be greater risks from disaster, war, disease, and terrorism.

The Military-Industrial Establishment helps us fulfill these roles automatically. It is our insurance policy against a whim of the people that would weaken our defense and stabilization forces in exchange for this or that social program. It is an important part of our national grand strategy.

Without our State-Automating 5GW, the world would be transformed. Security guarantees would be meaningless. The nineteenth-century world of great power politics would come back, as global competition would be between equals without any power capable of global intervention. This world would not necessarily be catastrophic, but it would be tremendously risky. There is no other realistic threat in the next four to eight years that presents so much uncertainty and risk as the breaking of the iron triangle.

A harmonization of government spending with the people's will—an outbreak of democracy that overwhelms the iron triangle of politicians, beltway insiders, and job-seeking voters, is the greatest threat in the Age of Obama.

IDEAS AND STRATEGIES FOR A MORE SECURE FUTURE

MICHAEL TANJI

To a certain extent any book that purports to solve problems tends to lean towards being a laundry list of recognizable and readily understood tasks that if dutifully attended to should lead to global peace and harmony, or some semblance thereof. The primary difference between this effort and most works is that we eschew any pretense that a fixed agenda is a worthwhile endeavor. Any problem that could be solved so straightforwardly would have been taken off the global to-do list by now, so either our problems are simple enough but our solutions woefully inadequate, or these are problems too complex to address within generally accepted theories and practices.

The idea that these are simple problems that we make unnecessarily complicated—either through our own obtuseness or ulterior motives—is not without justification. There are both base and sophisticated reasons for not solving problems, or at least not solving them right away or in a given fashion. Then there are the failures and shortcomings of national and international institutions that fail to adapt to changing dynamics, that adopt the worst traits of bureaucracies, and attract the wrong people for all the wrong reasons. Let's face it: the list of failures by national and international institutions, when they were needed most, could fill its own book. The ineffectual gasps of such institutions and those that support them portend an age when what passed for authority and responsibility fades away to be replaced by a system that few who walk the halls of power anywhere fully appreciate. As has been pointed out recently in other works, the world is increasingly flat and systems that are truly local or closed are few, far between, and wildly inadequate for the demands of the age.

The approach here then is less to prescribe specific fixes for discrete problems, but to characterize an environment that, if constructed in a sound and robust fashion, will make it easier to deal with the problems at hand. Should solutions evade us, our new construct should make it easier to withstand the shocks and perturbations that would overcome more rigid, traditional systems. To that end we view this effort as something unique: a solutions platform that incorporates ideas and strategies—some familiar, some downright disruptive—that is much less about form and largely about function. In particular, a platform with functionality that scales from the local to the international level.

It is this scalability that is critical to dealing with the threats of the future. As noted in the previous section, past international problems can have a very personal impact. As anyone who is familiar with national-level responses to various attacks, disasters, and adverse natural conditions is aware, expecting the government to make you whole in a timeframe measured in anything less than weeks is ludicrous. As theorist and strategist John Robb points out, we are entering an age of "superempowerment" where it is entirely realistic to expect the individual to compete on par with the group or even the state.[116] Likewise it is imperative that we develop solutions that work on an individual level if success—or at least survival—is a goal.

We start by thinking about thinking, which is something both sides of the political and policy making spectrum could benefit from. Understanding why we draw the conclusions we do, the errors we make, and the fixes we could implement are an enlightening exercise that is inherently valuable yet rarely undertaken. Too often avoiding the mistakes of the past is code for "not doing what the last guys did," but that's not change, that's intentional ignorance.

---

[116] John Robb, *Brave New War* (New Jersey: John Wiley & Sons Inc., 2008).

With our decision-making processes adjusted or at least enlightened, we turn our attention to some of the inherent flaws in the system we are currently operating in. The United States isn't going away any time soon, but the power and influence she will wield going forward is going to be impacted severely if we cannot find a way to adapt our nation-state construct into something that can more readily deal with the increasingly dangerous non-state actor problem. We are not alone in this predicament and conglomerations of nation-states are not networks battling networks, they are a hodgepodge.

Granted, there are situations where the power of a nation and its associated mechanisms come in handy, and dealing with strategic threats is certainly one of them. Those who would rain death from above or via other means on a cataclysmic scale—the remotely sane ones at least- are unlikely to have entirely dismissed the potential impact of being on the business end of the full force and attention of a superpower. Ensuring that we explain and execute policies along a clear and decisive force continuum is still the soundest way to deal with rational actors.

Increasingly though, the nation's and world's problems are found in the virtual realms. It is these environments that have posed some of the most significant challenges to the national security establishment yet they also remain issue areas that are the least understood and receive the least serious attention and resources. One man alone cannot plunge the world into nuclear winter, yet it was not all that long ago that one man could have broken the networks of the world.[117] You cannot exactly compare the potential impacts of the events, but on questions of scope and scale (vice destruction and death) how is it that we have the

---

[117] Wired Magazine, November 2009, Secret Geek A-Team Hacks Back, Defends Worldwide Web (http://www.wired.com/techbiz/people/magazine/16-12/ff_kaminsky?currentPage=all)

policies and mechanisms in place to stop the former event from occurring, but stopping the latter is an entirely ad hoc process? Our multiple entries in this issue area are intentional: despite billions invested to date, and billions more to come, we still do not have a comprehensive strategy for addressing technological issues of national import.

More than the medium used to communicate, the messages we send across the air and wire are increasingly important not only for their content, but because our words reach farther, faster, and deeper than ever before. There are strong, legitimate concerns that our government not disseminate "propaganda" (in the worst sense of the word) at all, much less to her own people, but in an age when all communication is global and instantaneous, are decades-old rules on what constitutes domestic vs. a foreign audience valid? Is fear of a massaged message grounds for not communicating at all?

Success in dealing with present and future threats means discarding the status quo. Holding the line in any fashion in our policies and institutions isn't even a stop-gap anymore, it's a sure-fire way to ensure you backslide into a potentially unrecoverable condition. Those interested in reducing threats are not entertaining models or approaches that are dusted-off, re-treaded solutions of the past; they are contemplating approaches that are downright disruptive in nature, because if there is anything the last few years has shown us, it is how easily we ourselves are disrupted by sufficiently original thinking and bold action.

Finally we consider what it means to prepare for and execute a true strategy of change for the future. Such grand strategy is rarely implemented outside of war and even then difficult to understand much less implement when most people and communities are focused on the hear-and-now or at best a given lifetime. True, lasting, impactful change isn't measured in units most of us are comfortable discussing. Epochal thoughts are considered grandiose at best if not outright lunatic, but while we often speak of the end of various political, technological, societal eras, few talk about intentionally starting one.

President Obama wrote of "Change We Can Believe In" and we will know that his administration is serious about changing the way security problems are solved by its early actions in the issue areas described herein. Already that start is questionable given the well-known roster of persons being bandied about for key positions: none are names you would associate with change, reform, or progress in any practical fashion. As various observers have pointed out, many of the selections made to date have been based not on personal loyalty or political affinity, but largely their functional acumen: people who know how the wheels of government work *in the fashion we are trying to cast off.* What we have not seen as this text is being drafted are any selections of individuals who have demonstrated a willingness to entertain new ideas or gone out on a limb and actually tried implementing them. Re-treads from past administrations have their uses if your goal is the status quo but they will not get us to our destination; for that the leader of the free world will have to seek out and appoint those for whom the realization of ideas in service to the public is not a zero-sum game. People who view change not as another way to stick it to the other side, but as a means to leave behind a better agency, a better system, a better community, a better world, than the one they found. Change we can believe in with regards to the nation's most pressing security problems will come from those who are essentially beyond politics. They may not be apolitical by any stretch but they are focused on the pertinent issues and driven in their resolve to find solutions that keep people alive, safe and free.

PREPARING ONE'S MIND TO SEE

ART HUTCHINSON

Metacognition is one of the foremost attributes separating humans from animals. (In rough terms, it's the ability to think about thinking). We have the capacity to consider not merely what we are seeing, but to choose how we go about seeing. We can posit and then explore hypothetical possibilities that we may be failing to see or credit and to which we may need to pay greater heed going forward. We can reflect on our processes for analyzing and making sense of the information we take in and, lastly, we can be deliberate in modifying our information acquisition behaviors and processing frameworks (our 'mental models') in pursuit of a goal.

Mental models not described and examined tend to lead to decisions that don't fit reality. (Think blindfolded child whacking at a birthday party piñata and hitting grandma instead). In this chapter, I'll explore why it's important to become adept at understanding and shaping our own (and especially our organization's) mental model(s) to accommodate a range of possible futures and why this capability is absolutely essential in times of high uncertainty, borderline chaos and step-function change. Towards the end, I'll explain a few time-tested metacognitive tricks and group processes for seeing what one may be missing and improving the power and precision of mental models for addressing complex futures in a more resilient manner.

The goal of a metacognitive, mental model modification effort might be limited in scope. ("How should I change my news-gathering habits to generate higher returns for my retirement portfolio next quarter?") Or it might be sweepingly complex. ("How can we get decision-makers across multiple organizations to develop a shared, richly-nuanced framework for dynamically assessing how non-Western worldviews may challenge our physical security, economic resilience and liberal, democratic values over the next 50 years?") At any level of abstraction however—e.g., individual or corporate, quantitative or holistic, discrete or open-ended,—the examination, amendment and practical use of mental models involves five basic components.

First is making mental models explicit: clarifying, in detail and with specific illustrations, how we currently see the world—including any internal, logical inconsistencies (there are always some). The second component involves enriching the methods we use to anticipate and/or envision change by constructing multiple new mental models (not forecasts) each designed to explain a set of potential future conditions. The third component involves comparing those new models against one another and against conventional wisdom. Fourthly, mental models impact strategy and tactics when one queries them, on an ongoing basis to see how they fit (or don't) with evolving conditions on the ground. (Think of checking a map against what one is seeing out the window.) Where opponents are involved (and they usually are), the process also entails a fifth element I'll term "meta-competitive.". That is: grasping a rival's way(s) of seeing the world faster than he is able to wrap his mind around yours.

In talking about our ability to see the future, it's worth reflecting on the more prosaic, literal way we think about seeing: with our eyes, within the electromagnetic spectrum. We humans can see only a very small part of it without the aide of scientific instruments. The fact that most wavelengths are invisible to the naked eye makes them no less real (just as pulling the covers up over one's head does not make one's room go away, even though children imagine it does). Tuning in to those invisible spectra (e.g., ultraviolet, infrared or X-rays) can literally shed light on some very interesting realities. The value of using specific, highly refined tools and techniques to help us see and work in alternative spectra is something we take for granted as beneficial. That ability has proven useful in a wide range of applications—respectively, for example, from semiconductor manufacturing to finding a lost skier out after dark in the back country to diagnosing his or her broken leg. In another part of the spectrum, my teenage kids take pleasure in cell phone ring-tones too high for me to hear with aging ears. Our family dog serves as a proxy indicator for that alternate reality.

When it comes to seeing other kinds of important, alternative patterns however—in society, geopolitics, international relations, economics, military strategy, etc—there is still a strong tendency to rely on our own inexplicit, experiential models, i.e., to attempt to see better within just one spectral range. We may make more effort to see (by collecting more data—the equivalent of squinting or using binoculars) but it is far less common to put on different lenses. We may run across circumstantial evidence of an alternative reality (my dog's funny look with the ring-tones, or my sensing heat from the stove with my hand) but we still filter out what our senses or past experience tell us is not worth our time. We may vow to put the things we don't understand in the back of our minds as possible, but typically those peripheral items get thrown in a mental junk drawer along with the stuff we judge to be simply loony.

Before we go any further however, let me be plain about something. Operating at this academic, "meta" level—challenging our capacity for seeing rightly—is not an everyday endeavor. When the world is changing incrementally, and/or when the sphere in which we need to operate is relatively contained and homogeneous, there are good and valid reasons why a limited set of filters for seeing makes sense and why any effort to overhaul them should be approached with great caution. Our mental models are built up over a lifetime, shaped and ingrained by hard-won experience. They have, by definition, gotten us where we are and, if we're happy with what that place is, we may cherish our mental models (and rightly so!) because their wisdom helps us make better decisions within a stable context. To the extent that they serve us well, we trust them implicitly and there is little need to examine them.

Within a particular context, our mental models improve, 1) the speed at which we can make sense of (and formulate reactions to) what's going on around us, 2) the appropriateness of our response and, 3) our ability to communicate at higher bandwidth with others who share the same or similar mental models. The broad platform of Judeo-Christian values and worldview underpinning much of what we call Western Civilization is just one example of a widely shared mental model that went virtually unnoticed for centuries because its basic precepts were seldom challenged. Operating within it made it possible to assume many things and thus be more efficient—not spending time on items such as the concept of the individual, how to charge interest on loans or what days of the week were for business.

Other contexts within which a single set of mental model "lenses" can provide a high level of efficiency in perception, communication and effective decision-making include companies, non-commercial institutions, political movements, nations, ethnic groups, social classes, career paths, functional roles and industrial sectors (among others). Most mental models, to varying degrees, are an amalgam of all of these filters, and that is one of the things that can make them cumbersome. You and I may talk about our views on issues and trends, but it takes a lot of time and effort (plus a common "language" for discussing it) to talk in terms of how those views inform our beliefs about future events. I'll get back to that point in a moment.

In fact, any shared context can develop powerfully (and then become taken for granted) within a bounded set of environmental conditions. Even if that context is broad and hazy (e.g., "the free market system plus relative economic prosperity") the benefits of sharing a mental model can be enormous, while the impediments to working beyond its bounds can be forbidding. The "soft," human-level difficulties Germany faced in re-integrating after the Berlin Wall came down in 1989 are one example. Two groups of people had a great deal in common (language, history, culture, geographic proximity, even family ties) but were separated abruptly and arbitrarily. Like Darwin's observations of bird species on remote islands, the mental models of East and West Germans after being split for 28 years (or 44, depending on how one counts)— their ways of seeing and thinking about a vast array of fundamental issues—might as well have originated on different planets.

Similarly, working with clients on Wall Street, I'm struck more each year by how few have any gut sense for what it felt like to ride out the stock market crash of 1987—much less the grinding stagflation, bear market, and attempts at wage and price controls in the 1970s. Thirty years earlier, the same was said of those who lacked adult experience of the Great Depression or World War II— an evergreen, generational truism that reaches well beyond finance.

Some of the particulars of the ravening financial market conditions that began to emerge in late 2007 and metastasized throughout 2008 were unprecedented (they usually are). Without an internal model to quickly recognize broad emerging patterns however (making rough "this seems/feels like that" analogies with past experience) more raw information doesn't necessarily help. It may only serve to confuse. A deep knowledge and vivid sense of history can help in such situations, but these days it's the rare individual who, a) has gone that deep, b) can bring that insight to bear with precision and, c) can convince his or her colleagues.

Getting through such times without any personal precedent for how to interpret them, think rightly and behave differently is akin to the challenge of emerging from a cave into bright sunshine (or perhaps, vice versa in this case). Everything one needs to see is all around, but one is temporarily blinded by the radical change in lighting. It takes awhile for one's eyes to adjust and in some cases we may not have that luxury. Those who did have the ability to make sense of the sub-prime meltdown and its cascading after-effects were mostly long gone by the time it took place. The "lenses" worn by most in the financial industry simply were not adapted to the critical signals they most needed to see as I wrote this heading into 2009.

A related context that powerfully informs mental models (and thus our sense of threat and possibility) is the existence or non-existence of a particular set of technological capabilities. My grandfather found it remarkable that all his grandchildren were "working in computers" even though our career paths are as diverse as one can imagine. He had no sense of the vast range of things computers do—not the human creativity, productivity and connectedness they have made possible, nor the many new modes of time-wasting, fraud and depravity they have unleashed. He never fully understood my flying across time zones routinely (he did so once, in a car). And he couldn't shake the sense that an interstate phone call over five minutes was a luxury item. His blind spots around technology, regulation, wealth, work, and lifestyle made it hard to grasp how the world really "worked" when he left it at age ninety-seven. And yet, he was one of the first people I called after 9-11, grasping for ways to make sense. "So with two young kids, a mortgage and one low-paid job, what did you think, feel and do when you went to work on Monday, December 8th, 1941?", I asked him. "We just changed the faces on the bayonet practice dummies and went back to drills" he replied. Not politically correct, but it was helpful in winning the war. As Malcolm Gladwell has observed, one's "blink" response is often as good as what pundits may take years to figure out—provided one has the right model.

And so it's worth pausing to distill an important aspect of what it takes to see more clearly across a broad spectrum: experiential variety—either within a person or organization. (I'm deliberately avoiding the term "diversity" here because, a) it doesn't make all that much sense when applied to individuals and, b) it has come to imply many things with no relation to the kind of broad-spectrum (multi-lens) seeing capability we're talking about or, to paraphrase the Apple commercials: to "think different[ly]".) One of the most vibrant firms I ever worked with had the unusual characteristic of nearly equal numbers of professionals in every ten-year age bracket—from 20-something to 70-something. That made it more difficult to make some kinds of assumptions. Some conversations progressed fairly slowly; but it dramatically enhanced our ability to recognize emerging patterns and figure out how to address them.

The case for challenging established mental models (trying on different lenses through which to look at the world) can seem dubious when one clear, fixed rule-set is dominant. In a highly stable environment for example (think mid-Cold War era) it is only rational to tune our mental models to one environment and to its explicit and implicit rule sets and norms—to put on one set of highly polished worldview lenses. One mental model "wins" (compared to a more variegated set of fashion-forward colored contacts) because the individuals wearing them see super-clearly in the one spectrum of primary importance. They may overlook the significance of some peripheral realities that may become important later, but who cares in the heat of an existential conflict?

One illustration: terrorism by Islamic fundamentalists against Western interests was not unknown in the 1970s—or even the 1770's (go Google [Barbary pirates + "Thomas Jefferson"]. The existence of that phenomenon was obvious, even as its broader implications were perceived by most as just one issue among many. Since terrorism was part of but not central to the larger conflicts that defined those eras (at least for Americans) it was not a problem to open the F-stop and reduce the depth of field—ignoring the background in favor of shutter-speed and capturing the action in the foreground much more precisely.

The process of modifying mental models to better fit hypothetical circumstances (the ones in the background) can be slow and painful for individuals. It's even more daunting for teams and larger organizations. As a result, the tricks and processes I'm about to describe aren't often applied with much rigor or passion at the collective level unless the obsolescence of a previously dominant model has become manifest (or nearly so). The problem? By that point, one's strategic options have narrowed sharply. Modifying one's mental model after the surprise attack has occurred is too late.

This chapter rests on an assumption that we live in an environment that's changing faster, is more saturated with information and is more globally interdependent than ever before—and that it's not going back. One does not need to take a strong position one way or the other on whether such a world is structurally, culturally or even economically "flat" in order to accept that "wearing" a single, polished set of worldview lenses for a career (much less a lifetime) is no longer viable. Events originating well beyond what might once have been considered a discrete domain of analysis (e.g., a country, an industry, an organization, etc.) are now commonplace. In addition, the frequency of "step-function" change whether systemic or deliberate and sophisticated (meta-innovation on the very rules of engagement) makes the mastery of mental model adaptation progressively more necessary.

All of these justifications for metacognitive work hark back to the tragedy of the mythical Cassandra. Her curse was individual prescience combined with a perennial inability to persuade anyone to see what she saw or take her predictions seriously. One thinks, for example, of Manhattan U.S. Attorney Mary Jo White, who was characterized as a "Cassandra" for seeing the hazards of rigid rules for information-sharing between law enforcement and intelligence agencies that made it more difficult to piece together the elements of the 9-11 plot in advance—an exercise that became, in one tragic morning, forensic. Against such a backdrop, it should be apparent that any latent reluctance to examine and question mental models and their corresponding rule-sets is archaic. Someone is going to challenge them if only because they know that doing so may give them a competitive advantage.

The scenario work I've done with clients over two decades is rooted in this Cassandra effect: the precept that mental models strongly color what people believe is possible and therefore the kinds of potential problems and opportunities they are willing to see as valid—individually, collectively or, often, both.

The first step in working with mental models is making them explicit. We do this with our clients by developing a set of 120 to 180 hypothetical "headlines from the future," each with some accompanying, explanatory text. We call these 'events'. They're specific and time-delimited, designed to be plausible (but not obvious), challenging (but not outlandish). Many of them look like prediction market propositions (though the process, and its objectives are somewhat different): "Will a Nuclear Device Go Off in the Middle East Region Before 2010?" "Will China's GDP Growth Dip Below 2% Before 2015?" A properly-engineered event set "stakes out" a broad terrain of issues, pulling people into areas they may not know as much about, helping them to appreciate the broader fabric and pattern of the strategic landscape the whole group needs to see better. Getting there involves a small team writing 300 or more events from interviews and other research over a period of many weeks, then whittling it down. There is at least as much art as science to the process of getting it right.

By getting each member of the group to render a vote on each of these 120-180 events, we accomplish several important things. We develop a picture of what that group—and each individual—believes about the future in highly concrete terms. "Do you believe this will happen by this date? Yes or no?" They may be wrong. They may be at odds with one another. They may not have enough information to say ('I'm not sure" is an OK answer). For the first time, however, they are able to see a pixilated if imperfect image of what the results of their own mental model look like and what the results of the collective one tells them. It is, in essence, a mirror—usually with some big holes and cracks. Some of the stories it tells may make sense; others don't and that's the point. It sets up the tension for the next step: creating several new models that, while hypothetical, have more narrative coherence and explanatory power. These new models are, in effect, modular scenarios in that the potential story-lines are constructed from a common set of piece-parts, conceptually not unlike Tinker Toys.

The trick we use to help groups construct these new models is what I call "simulated hindsight": assume that a specific future "end state" has come about (a new business model, a new world order, a broad new rule-set of any kind) and work backwards. Assemble the story and key events that would had to have happened (future perfect past tense) to make it all coalesce. It's both more complicated and easier than it may sound. Developing a rich, tightly-written, plausible, challenging, internally consistent set of four or five end states takes some serious work and many judgment calls—a topic beyond the scope of this chapter. They're not meant to be perfectly prescient but to sketch the broad outlines of some "what-ifs" that a few folks are talking about, if only privately.

Why do we do it this way? Because working backwards is freeing. Most futurists, pundits and planners work within a today-forward framework: "What if this happened tomorrow and then this the next day and then this other thing the day after that?" (And so on.) Consciously or not, they filter out events they think are less plausible (or, worse, that they know perfectly well are quite plausible but that are not seen as very likely by management). Wanting to construct scenarios from events that seem likely, planners self-censor, leaving out some that might be game-changing but which, from the vantage of today, seem only marginally likely.

Take any surprise or major development in history and explain how it came about. Microsoft and Intel come to dominate the computer industry. Peace comes to Northern Ireland. Truman beats Dewey. China becomes an economic juggernaut. At one time, each of those things was seen as highly unlikely. Yet in hindsight, it's straightforward to identify key events that led to each conclusion. The noise level diminishes and one can tell the story of any major de facto development with at most a dozen or so illustrations. By simulating hindsight and playing the role of future historian looking back, it's possible to unleash the same kind of clear, sequential thinking about an end-state that is seen as 'highly unlikely' today.

The third step involves comparing event-based, modular scenarios to one another as well as to the base mental model of conventional wisdom. Some events may appear in more than one scenario. Others may be unique to one. A few key events may represent forks in the road. (If this happens, we're headed down this path; if it doesn't, then this other end state becomes much more likely.) In essence, what gets developed is a map. Key events serve as road signs.

Once one has developed a rich map of potential future terrain, the day-to-day process of reading news headlines becomes a much more focused, less frantic process—looking for evidence that key events (or close proxies) may be coming about. That's the fourth step. Children look at everything that goes by the car window, focusing attention almost at random. (It is no accident that they tend to get car-sick far more often.) Adult drivers, by contrast will look for specific signs and landmarks and ignore most of the others. The process is far more selective—matching the evolving landscape to a cartographic representation of it. We've had clients create so-called "war-rooms" (either virtual or physical) in which they've matched up headlines with these hypothetical event-based maps. They serve a function within some large organizations akin to that of a lost couple arguing over where they really are. Evidence-based querying against an agreed-upon map can resolve disagreements quickly and even become a means for rapid consensus-making around pre-considered strategic responses.

The final step that's useful in a competitive situation is a close cousin to war-gaming. At the front end, we might write one or more end-states from the competitor's point of view. What kind of world would they most want to live in? How would it work? What would it look like? Teams tasked with working out those scenarios with simulated hindsight invariably start to go native and understand a rival's thinking even when the specific competitor is not named. The other element of the meta-competitive use of scenarios involves working through them at the event level, thinking about what the rival's favored outcome might be on each one and how he might go about achieving it. The whole process is designed to work as a fractal. What keeps it to a manageable scope is the tendency of the event-based analysis to weed out large numbers of items previously thought to be worth tracking. One develops new better lenses for seeing but also a greater ability to focus tightly.

PARTING THOUGHTS

Are the mental models of individuals able to change faster than those of groups? Yes and no. We all know some stubborn stick-in-the-mud who just doesn't "get it.". (It's never us; it's always someone else.) Anecdotally, I know of more individuals who've had a "Damascus-road" 180-degree "a-ha!" moment, often within a workshop like I've described than I do groups or companies who have. Organizations change. They just don't often do it all that quickly. When one does, (e.g., Bill Gates' famous "Internet" memo), it tends to be a case of a powerful individual changing his mind, not evidence of the group turning quickly together.

Mental models are more often reflected in analytical tools and their outputs than they are challenged by them. Insights can definitely be had with quantitative tools, but sophisticated computer models, for the most part, tend to only amplify the force and reach of our brains. They do not, as a general rule, make us better able to "think different[ly]," change our gut instinct or instill deeply within us new ways of seeing the world, assessing its risks, plotting strategy or igniting innovation.

THE ISSUES OF NON-STATE ACTORS AND THE NATION STATE

SAMUEL P. LILES

In 1648, the theologically derived European states signed a binding peace accord known as the Westphalia Peace. In summary, the accord brought together much of the scholarship of the time into human rights language and created a substantial document within the treaty that would not end war as we know it, but did limit the scope of conflict substantially until 1914 and the beginning of World War 1. The concept of a nation state as a sectarian ruler, and thus abridging the power of the state and realizing the sanctity of human rights to religion and expression, as denoted in the treaty, were new ideas that the Continental Congress relied on to write the Declaration of Independence and later the Bill of Rights[118] (

A simple overview of the origin of nation states belies that the concept of sectarian sovereign nation and specifically Catholic ruled nations was a point of conflict in Europe in the 14th through 16th century. The treaty signed at Westphalia of course has changed and been updated throughout the years, but the basic tenets of setting nations as having borders and rules of conduct in peace and war has colored the political landscape ever since.[119] It would be outside the scope of this paper to lay out all of the issues with the treaty, but it created the framework for dispute and was rapidly evolved into alliances and even trade agreements. The treaty is a principal ancestor to the League of Nations, and the United Nations.[120]

---

[118] Gross, L. (1948). The Peace of Westphalia, 1648-1948. *The American Journal of International Law*, 42(1), 20-41.
[119] *Ibid.*
[120] *Ibid.*

Understanding the origin of nation states and the rise of non-state actors in the global environment better informs risk analysis for homeland security. Whereas the nation state has almost 350 years of contemporary history, the non-state actor has uncountable years of experience in conflict. The nation state was created in a desire to reduce and limit the scope of conflict due to religion and economics. Though not perfect, it became an arbiter in restraining the theocracies and monarchies of the time and later defining the sectarian state. The basic ideas of the treaty and the follow on agreements was to create a substantial principle to mitigate overt conflict and civilian casualties. Unfortunately this also created a substantial tension on the inter-reliance of nations and of course never stopped war completely. With the history of 350 years of diplomacy being that between sovereign nations it then comes as no surprise that the mechanisms of international law and diplomacy have little in the way of tools to deal with insurgents, transnational criminals, errant corporations, or international terrorists. The national law enforcement systems are not set up to deal with high-risk international terrorists, and the national militaries can not handle the domestic consequences of mitigating the conflict at home.

A good example of the difference between nation states warring and non-state versus nation state conflict is the Vietnam War. There were two Vietnams (North and South), and there were two wars. The first war was the North Vietnamese versus the South Vietnamese as a conventional war. The second war was the Viet Cong insurgency that harassed and harried the citizens and troops in South Vietnam. The second war was being won by normal counter-insurgency methods, but the second war was almost ignored because of those counter-insurgency activities.[121]

---

[121] Sarkesian, Sam C. and Scully, William. *U.S. Policy and low intensity-conflict: Potentials for military struggles in the 1980's.* (New York: Transaction Books, 1981).

It is important to understand the conflict that arises from war other than war and the nature of low intensity conflict. Low intensity conflict (LIC) was first euphemized in congressional testimony and then enacted in defense appropriations spending bills. Though circular "war other than war" was the phrase coined to discuss the types of conflict that exist short of a declaration of war as mandated within the United States Constitution. For our discussion we will use LIC as the primary term which spans conflict from standard law enforcement actions to small wars and counter insurgency activities. Since war is a continuum there is overlap and LIC may exist within the domain of war, but war rapidly reaches outside the scope of LIC (*Low-intensity conflict: The pattern of warfare in the modern world*, 1989).

TERRORISM AND THE NATION STATE

The treaty at Westphalia in 1648 set the domain of the nation state as a geographic entity. Prior to this point, nations were conglomerates of political entities and sovereign in rare occurrences but often beholden to the religious entities of the time. It has been argued in numerous government documents that most terrorism has a political component and that almost always is state sponsored at some level. Whether talking about Iranian sponsored terrorism during the fall of the Shah of Iran and the hostage crisis of that era, or if talking about Libyan sponsored terrorism and the bombing of Libya by the United States as reprisal in 1986. Terrorism has existed as a tactic of conflict for a long time and as a political tool since Nikita Krushchev endorsed "wars of national liberation" in 1961. This is the point at which terrorism made the leap from localized to globalized as a tool of national will.

The principles of conflict in the dichotomy of non-state aggressors and nation states is important to understand as is the

---

Thompson, Loren B. *Low-intensity conflict: The pattern of warfare in the modern world.* (Lexington, Massachusetts: Lexington Books: 2008).

effect it has on strategy. The non-state actor is one that may exist in a geographic region or multiple geographic regions acquiring through private fund raising monetary support, and the state-sponsored actor may derive support from national treasuries and still exist in multiple geographic regions. The principle is that the state may sponsor terrorist cells. This is not as unusual as it sounds. The principles of terrorism and LIC have been clouded by political rhetoric but the realities are that terrorist cells and organizations are perfectly suited to proxy conflict between super powers that pay at least some homage to the international rules of war. As such the intention is to use counter-terrorist tools and the doctrine of LIC to keep terrorism based on foreign shores and away from the United States. This would seem to play into the political needs of adversaries as the idea of a terrorist is to keep the United States in pain but not so painful as the full might of the military may be used to strike down the terrorist and any sponsors . The term "small wars" has been used in the past to break the euphemism of LIC and to remove the softened tone of LIC when dealing with policy makers. Small wars doctrine can trace its history in United States military circles all the way back to the United States Marine Corps *Small Wars Manual* published after the Banana Wars and published originally in the early 1930's.

Homeland security needs to be informed as to the ideas and political issues of the nation-state at war and how non-state actors would be handled under the rule of law. Civil defense has been an activity of homeland security in the past and disaster relief is still the provender of homeland security. Each of these roles are for protection within the United States from foreign and domestic violence. The national infrastructure and intelligence apparatus should be providing the local and state communities with appropriate analysis on which to secure and defend the homeland.

The Westphalian concept of nation state specifically creates a situation where conflict is nation against nation rather than nation against corporation or citizen. The nation state model supported national militaries vying against each other in conflict. The concept that a non-state actor would even have the ability to wage war against the nation state would not have been considered a possibility and the successful prosecution of an asymmetric war by non-state actors against a nation state not even within the realm of reason.[122]. Of course, with the advent of Al Queda terrorist type groups and radicalized religious extremism, technologically sophisticated adversaries, nation states that never prepared to battle adversaries not of their own type has left those nation states struggling to understand the new conflict.

Homeland security is inextricably linked to the concept of a nation state and as such the rise of non-state actors as adversaries will also cause problems. The legal, moral, and ethical base of the nation state precludes waging wars on citizens and the term terrorist when applied precludes Geneva Convention protection and rules of war protections for the terrorist. The disharmony within the legal frameworks can cause issues between the nation states as declaring somebody a terrorist or declaring a fundamental military branch of another nation a terrorist organization can create global political issues outside of the conflict .[123]

HOMELAND SECURITY AND THE NATION-STATE VERSUS TERRORISM

The all hazards approach of homeland security allows for a response to the actual incident of terrorism and the coordinated planning thus becomes appropriate to the actual incident. That National Response Framework (NRF) and the National Incident Management System set new priorities in responding to terrorism depending on the vector of the threat. The homeland security

---

[122] Robb, J. *Brave new war: The next stage of terrorism and the end of globalization.* (Hoboken, New Jersey: John Wiley & Sons, 2008.)
[123] Lesser, Hoffman, Arquilla, Ronfeldt, & Zanini. *Countering the new terrorism.* (Santa Monica, CA: RAND. 1999).

response when mitigating all hazards allows the different agencies to share information in a variety of ways and through a variety of tools prior to an incident. This hazy description of all hazards approach appears to be an inclusive rather than an exclusionary approach to the future protection of the United States. The response mechanism can be anything from public awareness campaigns to military interdiction on foreign lands.

The concept of homeland security as civil defense is a direct result of the overriding concept of a nation. When you look at the National Guards of each state as separate entities the nation takes on a fragmented approach. Realizing this, the federalization of the National Guards and standardization has created mission specific organization within the Guard system capable of responding in a much more coordinated effort than a single state's systems would have as capability[124]. The secondary effect this has is to spread out the capability of different state units across the much larger national geography.

Anti-terrorism and counter terrorism are not the same thing. [125] The physical protections and hardening of facilities against attack is anti-terrorism while the hunting down and interdicting of terrorists before they commit an act is counter terrorism.[126] Homeland security has specific roles of mitigation in anti-terrorism measures and these reflect inwards toward the nation-state. Anti-terrorism measures effectively are insurance not against terrorist events, but against the effects of terrorist acts. Counter terrorism has a decidedly outward looking aspect from the perspective of the nation state. That is not to suggest that terrorism cannot be homegrown and of a domestic nature. The terrorist though is perceived to have left the fold of the nation-state and be an external

---

[124] Gallagher, C. J. J. Low-intensity conflict: A guide for tactics, techniques, and procedures. Mechanicsburg, PA: Stackpole Books, 1992.
[125] *Ibid.*
[126] Sarkesian, *supra.*

entity. When the terrorist is foreign many of the rules of war do not apply. There are differences in how each nation applies the rule of law towards terrorist suspects, but in general the normal criminal law of the United States is applied when prosecuting a terrorist.[127] There are some examples such as tracking down financing and sponsorship where specific laws have been put in place to find terrorists but those are outside the scope of this discussion.

Internal emergency relief is a primary mission for the homeland security and within the United States the Federal Emergency Management Agency (FEMA). The activities of FEMA are generally considered to be domestic in nature but some of the same organizational activities that FEMA coordinates are used internationally to assist in foreign disasters.

When the domestic security elements of homeland security are used to combat terrorism you can infer that national security informs policy. The issue is that in many ways the nation state must be as flexible as the non-state actor or specifically terrorist. As stated previously the traditions of national entities specifically are set up to preclude actions against non-state actors. That would suggest that the tradition is in contrast to the realities of current conflict and in direct conflict with providing real security. This has caused what is perceived to be policy gap and error in some ways of handling terrorism. Because of the traditional roles being in conflict with the current realities the differing states have differing ways of dealing with terrorism. That vague statement begets a horrible truth that the nation-state may be poorly suited for actually fighting terrorism anywhere but domestically.

CONCLUSIONS AND RECOMMENDATIONS

Low intensity conflict is a result of the Westphalia treaty in many ways. The limits imposed in that treaty set up a framework of

---

[127] Gallagher, *supra.* and Lesser, *supra.*

national dispute resolution up to and including war, but the limits imposed created a power vacuum. From that framework over three hundred years ago the descendant documents of that have been agreements like the Geneva Convention, and the League of Nations. In some ways the current conflicts between nation states and radicalized religious or environmental groups using terrorism and a tool of social change are a refutation on the concept of a nation state. The concept of terrorism could be considered a return to more feudal political patterns and especially in the case of religious motivated terrorism a return to the period prior to the Treaty of Westphalia.

Low intensity conflict as counter-terrorism was not expected at the time of the Westphalia treaty though we know that Caesar considered the taking of hostages to be a political act when conquering tribes.[128] When considering the roles of nation states and how terrorism inflicts itself on nations there needs to be a flexible, sustainable, mobile response. A thread through the literature not discussed exactly but alluded to in many places is that law-enforcement and military response to terrorism both as anti-terrorism and counter-terrorism is an ineffective method of reducing risk. Law enforcement is not agile enough and does not carry enough authority to successfully counter terrorist acts though it is fairly successful in prosecuting suspected terrorists once they are caught (after the act). The military though is a blunt instrument with special operations capability but the political baggage of working in foreign lands and the rules of war combined handicap its efforts. Whereas law enforcement is successful at prosecution the military under many restraints is not as successful at finding and fighting terrorists (though the military has had successes).

For homeland security, law enforcement and not the military are the primary tools for fighting internal threats due to the national

---

[128] Gallagher, *supra.*

laws in place restraining military actions. Though the issue of military action being restrained is not necessarily as true as widely suspected *posse comitatus* does apply and most respect it beyond the actual restrictions it imposes. In any case, the restraint is negligible in importance as law enforcement rarely is in a position to stop a terrorist act entering the final phase. Military commanders and federal agencies, though, have a wealth of tools that can be used to combat terrorism, and these should be explored. The Department of Homeland Security Fusion Centers are an excellent start. Another idea is to embed law enforcement officers with military and national intelligence agencies to gain a new perspective on the needs of law enforcement. The intelligence process is a loss-full process where the gross amount of data produced and collected and analyzed to the point of a net product that is substantially more refined but devoid of a lot of content. In that lost content of the analysis process law enforcement can often find valuable information that has been filtered.

This paper is written at a fairly high level in an effort to draw some value from the concept of a nation and how that might inform domestic security without devolving into a philosophical diatribe. It appears often that when talking about security we talk about personal security and protecting the citizen rather than the state[129] This is an interesting paradox as the concept of a nation is to protect the nation and sometimes at the expense of the citizen. To put this in perspective it is now considered politically to be feasible to protect 300 million American citizens as a duty of Homeland Security. If that expectation reaches the state of reality only failure can result.

The lesson we can draw from pertinent literature is that the nation is an inflexible, restricted, repressed, and powerful entity. The non-state actor has none of the negatives of the nation-state

---

[129] Lesser, *supra.*

and many of the positives minus the power.[130] Thus the asymmetric warfare concept flourishes. Terrorism exists in even the most heavily policed states, so the idea that we can stop terrorism entirely even through totalitarian or dictatorial rule is a lie. The truth is that by realizing the issues that the nation-state will have in dealing with terrorism, more flexible tools to combat terrorism can be realized, and with international consent terrorism can be defined and dealt with in a coordinated and effective fashion.

---

[130] Barno, D. Challenges in fighting a global insurgency. *Parameters* (Summer), 15-29. 2006.

THE FUTURE OF MISSILE DEFENSE POLICY

TOM KARAKO

On the day after Election Day, November 5, 2008, Russian President Dmitri Medvedev presented President-elect Barack Obama with actions which had all the appearances of bullying. Medvedev announced plans to deploy SS-26 Iskander missiles to Kalingrad if the United States did not retreat from pursuing ballistic missile defense programs with Poland, a former Warsaw Pact country within range of even the short range missiles. Only a few months previously, Medvedev fired a number of SS-26 Iskander and SS-21 Tochka missiles against civilian targets in the former Soviet republic and now independent country of Georgia. One missile hit an oil pipeline; another hit downtown Gori, killing five people.

Medvedev simultaneously presented the President-elect with an alternative of removing the unpleasantness if the United States would only comply with its wishes as regards Poland: "But we are ready to abandon this decision to deploy the missiles in Kaliningrad if the new American administration, after analyzing the real usefulness of a system to respond to 'rogue states', decides to abandon its anti-missile system." Ballistic missiles, it appears, remain an important tool in both diplomacy and defense policy.

Designed to defend against Iran, the ten ground based interceptors intended for deployment in Poland (but still years away from deployment) would pose no real threat to the free ride of Russia's nuclear forces toward the United States, whether launched from Russian ICBM fields or submarines. The missile-rattling of Russia seems as much a foreign policy question of who gets to play in the Eastern European sandbox as a defense policy question of strategic significance. The United States has, however, entered into a number of agreements with allies and NATO over the last eight years. Russia's attempt to bully President-elect Obama raises the question whether the United States will abandon the course of diplomatic cooperation on missile defense thus far taken with allies, or whether long term strategic interests will be traded for the short term appeasement of countries like Russia.

The missile defense policy questions facing the new Obama administration in 2009 are very different from those which faced the Bush administration in 2001 or the Clinton administration in 1993. Over the last eight years, some limited defenses have been deployed and numerous agreements have been signed with allies for technological cooperation on missile defense, including Great Britain, South Korea, Japan, India, Australia, the Czech Republic, and Poland. NATO has renewed interest in supporting the bilateral program with Poland. In the face of Iranian missile production and testing numerous middle eastern countries are now standing in line to purchase short- and medium-range defenses. Dutch and Japanese ships have been involved in the actual testing of sea-based programs. The Japanese are now licensed to produce Patriot interceptors of their own, have deployed several such batteries. The United States has deployed a radar in Israel, and helps Israel expand and improve its own Arrow interceptors. Talks exist with numerous other countries as well.

With such widespread interest and support, missile defense cannot be characterized as a merely unilateral effort on the part of the United States. Russia, of course, has maintained its own limited missile interceptors around Moscow since the 1960s, and Israel continues to upgrade its layered system of interceptors.

Barring a dramatic retreat from these diplomatic arrangements by the Obama administration, the United States and its allies will probably continue to retain some missile defense programs. The question, however, is what kind of missile defense programs we will have, and how much of them. At the level of the budget, near-term programs may be retained at the expense of longer-term research programs. At the level of diplomacy, the new administration will have to evaluate cooperative efforts with other countries within range of Iranian missiles will continue. During the presidential campaign, Obama pledged support for missile defense, but emphasized that it be cost effective, be technologically sound, and not divert resources from other national security issues. What this will mean as a matter of policy and for specific programs remains to be seen.

To gain perspective on the missile defense challenges facing the United States today, it is worth reviewing how we got here. March 23, 2008 marked the twenty-fifth anniversary of Ronald Reagan's speech announcing the Strategic Defense Initiative (SDI), a research and development program designed to render obsolete the ballistic missiles which served as delivery vehicles for nuclear and other weapons of mass destruction.

At one time we supposed we might have peace and stability with the Soviet Union on the basis of mutual vulnerability to missile attack. This idea of purely offensive deterrence with the threat of nuclear retaliation, forwarded by Thomas Schelling, was made policy by Secretary Robert Strange McNamara in the early 1960s. What began in the Kennedy administration persisted in Republican and Democratic administrations alike. In 1972, the United States under Richard Nixon entered into the ABM Treaty, pledging to remain vulnerable to missile attack, and to hope that mutual vulnerability would bring security.

Unfortunately, this purely offensive form of deterrence had no answer or plan in the event that deterrence should fail. It was, as Keith Payne has recently written, a great "gamble." Reagan believed it more sensible to try to defend lives with a shield than to avenge them with a nuclear sword. Rethinking the old Cold War policies of mutually assured destruction (MAD), he saw that deterrence could be strengthened with defenses which made an enemy doubt a missile attack would succeed.

Over the last eight years the Bush administration has taken important first steps toward national missile defense. It withdrew from the ABM Treaty in 2002 and made tremendous progress testing and deploying missile defenses, two things Reagan did not do. During the first Gulf War, the Patriot interceptor gained fame for its engagements with Iraqi Scuds. Missile defense could be done after all, it seemed. During the second, Operation Iraqi Freedom, an improved Patriot interceptor was launched against nine Iraqi missiles, and all nine were destroyed. The Bush administration began deployment in 2004 of limited sea-based and ground-based interceptors. By the end of 2008, the United States will have eighteen Aegis missile defense ships, and over 25 ground based interceptors will have been deployed in silos at Fort Greely, Alaska and Vandenberg Air Force Base, California.

Current programs deserve much praise, but nevertheless fall short of SDI in important ways. Reagan envisioned a defense which was strategic, oriented to stopping the very most an enemy could threaten. SDI emphasized interceptors pre-positioned in low earth orbit. Space-based interceptors formed the primary line of defense, supplemented by sea- and land-based interceptors. By the early 1990s SDI had advanced to the level of a major defense acquisition program a constellation of small space-based interceptors. The Brilliant Pebbles concept promised a cost-effective way to destroy missiles in their ascent or boost phase, when they are most visible and most vulnerable. As the Missile Defense Agency's historian has documented, the program was cut for political reasons just as it was nearing the deployment phase. Its technologies were however successfully space-tested by the Clementine and Astrid programs in 1994.

Some hesitation about space defenses comes from the idea that space is a weapons-free preserve. But the high ground of space is merely an extension of strategic geography, and has long been "weaponized." Armies project power on land, navies on the high seas, and aircraft in the atmosphere. Satellites and missiles do so above the atmosphere. Satellites which surveil the enemy or send GPS coordinates to a warfighter are no less weapons because they do not go "boom." If a satellite in orbit helps direct a laser-guided bomb to a target in Afghanistan, in exactly what sense is space not weaponized?

All ballistic missiles travel through space, and it makes sense to intercept them from and in space. Putting interceptors closer to the paths of these missiles shortens the distance they must travel and widens the window of reaction time. Pre-orbited interceptors are pre-accelerated to 8km/sec, and do not require a massive booster rocket. Any surface-based system, by contrast, retains the physical challenge of needing to be accelerated at a moment's notice. In missile interception, seconds matter. Basing in space buys time.

Orbital basing also increases the ability to destroy missiles in their boost phase. Unless very near the launch site, ground-based interceptors cannot reach missiles in their boost phase if launched inland. Orbits know no political boundaries, so orbiting interceptors could potentially reach missiles in boost phase even if launched deep inside Pakistan or Iran—or Russia, or China.

China and Russia have consistently objected to space-based defenses precisely because of their more robust capabilities. The ground-based systems that form the backbone of today's missile defense programs are less threatening to more sophisticated, faster, and numerous Russian and Chinese missiles. The 1999 National Missile Defense Act required defense against "accidental, unauthorized, or deliberate" missile launch—there was no asterisk saying that this only meant certain kinds of missiles. Even without the ABM Treaty, missile defense policy which excludes space-based defenses remains MAD-compliant with respect to Russia and China. Our competitors' objections remain internalized in American domestic politics. Space-based interceptors are now treated as the third rail among missile defense programs: we seem self-deterred from touching them. An Obama administration which began to reexamine how space can better serve American defense policies would break from years of stagnation and atrophy.

Deliberately excluding the most robust defenses also makes defending against rogue state missiles more difficult. Today's ground-based interceptors in Alaska or California could not defend against a North Korean missile launched from a ship off the coast of Los Angeles. Ground-based interceptors in Poland could not reach an Iranian missile in its boost phase. One must not mistake recent advances to mean that we already have in place the kind of defenses needed to meet the growing threat. At the same time, the deployment of radars in both Israel and in the Czech republic would help in the detection of an Iranian-launched missile. Honoring the bilateral agreements and negotiations made thus far would also respect the widespread interest in missile defense among friends and allies.

If deliberate vulnerability ever made sense as a means to security, it makes even less sense now. Iran continues to develop its Shahab series, North Korea its Taepo Dongs. The Pentagon's annual report released in February notes that China continues to increase and modernize its ICBM force. Russia is deploying new land- and submarine-launched ICBMs specifically designed to overcome the current American ground-based midcourse interceptors.

One may defend the modesty of the current approach on the ground it is imprudent to irritate our strategic competitors in a time of war. But we should have no confusion about the degree to which hostile missiles retain a free ride to the American homeland.

Let us admit that we intend to remain vulnerable to even accidental and unauthorized missiles coming from Russia or China. The path of deliberate minimalism is deterred from boldly pursuing the most effective missile defense systems. Such paralyzing self-deterrence did not characterize the thought of Reagan or SDI, although it is true that even Reagan did not withdraw from the ABM Treaty or actually deploy any systems.

As Secretary of State Rice remarked in February 2008, "It is true that the United States once had a Strategic Defense Initiative, a program that was intended to deal with the question of the Russian strategic nuclear threat. This is not that program. This is not the son of that program. This is not the grandson of that program."

This is true. Twenty five years later, the "S" has been dropped from "SDI." We have missile defenses and the capability to have much more, but their progress has been deliberately underdeveloped. The Chinese anti-satellite intercept in 2007, using a ballistic missile to spectacularly destroy an aging weather satellite, reminded us of the intimate connection between missiles and space as well as the vulnerability of the satellites on which we depend for communication, reconnaissance and navigating our automobiles. What will it take to put the "S" back into how we think about space and missile defense policy? Should not the United States pragmatically pursue whatever defenses are most effective?

The next several years of the Obama administration will represent an important period for missile defense and space policy. It is doubtful the administration will reject all the progress made under both the Clinton and Bush administrations, both programmatically and diplomatically. At the same time some budget cuts may be expected. But what should be cut? How many programs, and of what kind? Today's robust Patriot PAC-3 and THAAD programs, while now seen as "near-term" systems ready for deployment, were at one time far-time research programs. It is important that today's far term research not be cut entirely, so that more capable systems will be there when we need them, as threats continue to evolve.

The new administration should begin by reviewing the growing missile threat with the seriousness and freshness of a Reagan, and confront the deliberate vulnerability that informs our current space and missile defense policies. Putting aside preexisting ideology and programs, missile defense policy should be keyed to the threat of a ballistic missile launched at the United States, our armed forces, or our allies, whether accidental, unauthorized, or deliberate. The numerous countries which have expressed interest in building, buying, or cooperating on missile defense efforts confirms that defense is not a unilateral program or interest unique to the United States. Positive policy change should begin by reevaluating the Cold War legacy of giving to Russia and China a veto on the most effective kinds of missile defense.

TOWARD A CONTEMPORARY DETERRENCE STRATEGY

CAROLYN LEDDY

One of the foremost security challenges of the 21st Century is the threat posed by weapons of mass destruction in the hands of rogue states or non-state actors who may not be deterred from using them against the United States or our allies. Confronting this exceptional challenge requires a comprehensive, robust, and flexible deterrence strategy. There is no one size fits all approach to deterrence.

The goal of deterrence is simple and straightforward— communicate to an adversary that the costs of a contemplated action will outweigh the expected gains. For most national security practitioners, deterrence discussions often recall thoughts of the Cold War struggle between the United States and the Soviet Union. The stark scenario of nuclear annihilation via Mutual Assured Destruction (MAD) was the common deterrence model of the Cold War era. Yet deterrence has become an increasingly complex, nuanced, and consequential endeavor in the face of 21st Century threats. The role of nuclear weapons in deterrence policy has diminished and innovative tools such as interdiction play an increasingly important role in combating the proliferation of weapons of mass destruction. Despite the multiplicity of tools, the ability to effectively deter perilous threats, especially the threat posed by WMD, remains an inexact science. Consequently, our nuclear deterrent must remain a reliable element of our deterrence policy.

In 2002, the Bush Administration articulated a dynamic and wide-ranging deterrence approach in the U.S. National Strategy to Combat Weapons of Mass Destruction or National Security Presidential Directive (NSPD-17). This strategy continues to serve as a model for successive administrations because it emphasizes a multi-faceted approach consisting of economic and financial; counterproliferation; scientific and technical; intelligence; diplomatic; and military tools. Economic and financial tools comprise traditional sanctions along with new and innovative measures to disrupt access to hard currency and international financial institutions by entities and/or individuals engaged in proliferation activities. The Bush Administration's Executive Order (EO) 13382, "Blocking Property of Weapons of Mass Destruction Proliferators and Their Supporters," is an example of one of these new financial tools. The E.O. enables the United States to block or freeze property and assets of weapons of mass destruction proliferators and their supporters. Counterproliferation measures to interdict weapons of mass destruction and related material and equipment harness a combination of diplomatic, legal, law enforcement and military tools. The interdiction of the *BBC China*—a German-owned ship seized carrying uranium centrifuge-related components destined for Libya's clandestine nuclear program—is the most often cited example of the potency of such successful efforts.

Scientific and technical capabilities are indispensable to strengthening our ability to detect and attribute the source of weapons of mass destruction and related material and equipment. Moreover, accurate and timely intelligence of an adversary's WMD activities, facilities, and capabilities is essential to sustaining diplomacy; improving scientific and technical capabilities; and conducting successful interdiction activities. It is widely accepted that intelligence failures related to Iraq's WMD programs complicated efforts to sustain multilateral cohesion. Diplomatic engagement, whether unilateral, multilateral or a combination of both, continues to be a forceful lever to induce or coerce a change in an adversary's behavior. Finally, keeping the full range of both defensive and offensive military options on the table is critical to efforts to dissuade, defend against, and mitigate the use of WMD.

Missile defenses and forward-deployed U.S. military forces stand as two of these critical deterrent tools. Successful deterrent efforts depend upon the availability and tailored combination of the above measures to the targeted adversary. Additionally, a critical element of an effective deterrence strategy that is often underappreciated is the role of a strong declaratory policy. In order to be effective, declaratory policy must articulate actions that are unacceptable and must hold the actors accountable for such actions. While maintaining a degree of ambiguity in terms of the exact response, it must be evident in declaratory statements that the costs of a contemplated action by an actor will outweigh any prospective gains. In order to be credible, a declaratory statement must say what you mean and mean what you say.

Likewise, consistency of declaratory statements over time is critical. An adversary must believe that articulated threats are credible. Drawing red lines and allowing them to be crossed undermines deterrence efforts not only with respect to the intended adversary but with other actors. These actors will observe how the United States acts to counter threats globally and draw lessons from the action or inaction. Consequently, the perception of capability and will on the part of the adversary of the willingness of the United States to use available deterrent tools plays an important role in the effectiveness of deterrence strategy. Establishing a clear red line and applying it consistently is essential to establishing and maintaining credibility over time. If the United States does not follow through on declaratory statements with actions then states and non-state actors will begin to question U.S. seriousness. The United States must demonstrate the willingness to follow through to impose the implied costs. The key to effective deterrence is finding the right balance between words and actions.

Moreover, U.S. deterrence policy must be adaptive. The threatened consequences must be targeted toward something that the adversary values. Preserving flexibility in deterrence policy enables the United States to adjust to respond to changing strategic circumstances.

The Bush Administration's declaratory statement with respect to North Korea provides an illustrative example of the difficulty of balancing policy statements with corresponding actions. It also highlights the prospective peril of inaction. Following North Korea's October 2006 nuclear test, President Bush issued a strong declaratory statement condemning the test. Moreover, the President's statement made clear that any attempt to transfer nuclear material would be met with a resolute U.S. response.

The North Korean regime remains one of the world's leading proliferators of missile technology, including transfers to Iran and Syria. The transfers of nuclear weapons or material by North Korea to states or non-state entities would be considered a grave threat to the U.S., and we would hold North Korea fully accountable of the consequences of such actions.

Less than a year following the issuance of the aforementioned statement, it was revealed that North Korea provided material assistance in the form a plutonium production reactor to a clandestine Syrian nuclear program. Regrettably, our interdiction efforts and intelligence assets proved insufficient to detect and disrupt the transfer of material and equipment necessary to construct the nuclear facility recently uncovered in Syria. Despite the egregious nature of activities in violation of this declaratory policy, the U.S. reaction was muted. No punitive actions were undertaken against North Korea.

The lack of response to North Korean proliferation seems to have undermined the credibility that the administration sought to establish through its strong declaratory statement. The deterrent tools, messages, and red lines applied toward North Korea not only affect the behavior of North Korea, but potentially other states and non-state actors. Undoubtedly, Tehran pays close attention to U.S.

policy toward North Korea, particularly U.S. actions to confront North Korean proliferation.

Iran's nuclear weapons program remains a significant challenge to effective deterrence against proliferation. Diplomatic engagement, including substantial inducements, has been the centerpiece of international deterrence efforts to confront Iran's nuclear weapons pursuit. Coercive and punitive tools have been important elements of this deterrence strategy. Successive rounds of unilateral and multilateral sanctions have tarnished Iran's international reputation and complicated access to the banking sector and hard currency. Nevertheless, Iran remains determined to acquire a nuclear weapons capability.

The United States continues to shift away from reliance upon nuclear weapons in deterrence policy toward a multi-faceted deterrence strategy that emphasizes proactive measures such as sanctions, interdiction activities, and scientific capabilities. This new multi-faceted deterrence concept is sensible and desirable; however, it is essential that our nuclear deterrent remain an effective and key component of our overall deterrence policy.

The traditional arms control community has long championed significant reductions in U.S. nuclear stockpiles, and many even advocate for the abolition of all U.S. nuclear forces. The central thesis rests on a simple moral axiom: the world would be a safer place without nuclear weapons. Indeed, the world would be more secure absent nuclear weapons; however, that is not the reality in which we live, where rogue states possess nuclear weapons and non-state actors are actively seeking to acquire a nuclear capability. Proponents of sharp and hasty reductions most often cite nonproliferation commitments undertaken by the United States as a party to the Nuclear Non-Proliferation Treaty (NPT) to validate their abolitionist calls. In particular, they harness their arguments to Article VI of the NPT which calls upon the nuclear weapons states (United States, Russia, China, France and the United Kingdom) to "pursue negotiations in good faith on effective measures relating to cessation of the nuclear arms race at an early date and to nuclear disarmament, and on a treaty on general and complete disarmament under strict and effective international control." Progress toward achieving nuclear disarmament and general and complete disarmament under Article VI is the responsibility of all NPT States Parties.

In fact, the arms control community contends that the United States is in violation of its commitments because reductions have not resulted in a more significant drawdown of nuclear forces. Despite this specious charge, the United States is in full compliance with NPT treaty commitments and has been faithfully reducing nuclear forces. Indeed, the United States has a concrete and impressive record of achievement with respect to its Article VI commitments. The United States partnered with Russia under the Moscow Treaty in 2002 to reduce its strategic nuclear warheads to unprecedented levels of 1,700–2,200.

It would not be overstating the case to assert that we are at a significant crossroads with respect to maintaining the safety, security, and reliability of our nuclear deterrent. The international drumbeat will only continue to grow louder for the abolition of nuclear weapons. Arms control proponents favor significant U.S. nuclear reductions and can now look to the White House under the leadership of President Obama for support in this regard. Recently, a bipartisan group of respected statesman—George P. Shultz, Henry Kissinger, William J. Perry and Sam Nunn—articulated a vision for a nuclear weapons free world.

As the chorus of the "movement toward zero" continues to grow louder, increasing widespread bipartisan support for reductions will most certainly be forthcoming. Continuing to drawdown the U.S. nuclear stockpile is prudent and consistent with international nonproliferation objectives. Yet further reductions must be part of an overall deterrence policy that is robust, dynamic, and accounts for the danger and unpredictability of the current strategic environment. Despite the persistence of perilous threats, a movement is underway to combine drastic reductions in nuclear forces with other arms control measures that will undercut rather than enhance U.S. deterrence efforts.

In addition to steep nuclear force reductions, arms control proponents seek to pursue ratification (again) of the still flawed Comprehensive Test Ban Treaty (CTBT); deny funding for safe and dependable nuclear weapons technology, including the Reliable Replacement Warhead (RRW) program; and undertake drastic cuts in missile defense activities. Such actions would be reckless, rather than responsible as arms control proponents assert. If implemented, these measures would undermine U.S. deterrence efforts and have far-reaching consequences for national and international security.

Consistent with U.S. alliance commitments and defense requirements, we must ensure the integrity and reliability of our nuclear deterrent. Having a number of tools at our disposal decreases reliance on any one particular and increases the overall chance for deterrence success in the face of daunting 21st Century threats.

AN INFORMATION AGE STRATEGY FOR GOVERNMENT INFORMATION TECHNOLOGY

MATTHEW BURTON

What is the perfect information technology solution to the threats mentioned in this book?

There isn't one solution to multiple threats. Rather than searching for a single solution, our national security community should adapt its IT procurement strategy to develop many solutions, each addressing a specific threat at the lowest possible cost.

The existing strategy is as follows: after being caught off guard by an unforeseen crisis--a terrorist attack, an outbreak of violence, or a surprise nuclear test--we reflect on our failure and identify a single cause. Maybe we didn't have enough information. Maybe we had too much information and couldn't sort through it all. Or maybe we had the right information but we didn't collaborate.

After pinpointing the cause we spend years—and tens of millions of dollars—trying to develop a handful of "Perfect Software Tools" to remedy the deficiency. Much of that time and money is spent on procurement bureaucracy: the first line of code is written after months of identifying requirements, issuing RFPs, waiting for bids, and awarding contracts.

This is an outdated strategy for two reasons. First, unforeseen crises are rarely the fault of a single deficiency. Fixing one problem while ignoring others is the equivalent of inviting strategic surprise. Second, the economics of innovation demand that creating a few tools will almost never solve our problem. After all, the vast majority of innovations fail. For every Google and Wikipedia there are hundreds of failed search engines and online communities.

Every high-dollar attempt at the "Perfect Software Tool" puts all of our eggs into the flimsiest of baskets.

If failure is so likely how do we ever build useful tools? By building more of them. And in order to do that, the price of each attempt must fall drastically. Instead of spending $10 million dollars on one tool, spend it on a thousand. The most valuable lesson for government IT decision makers is that real innovation requires experimenting with many different options.

A much lower cost per product is not as unrealistic as it may seem. Modern software need not be expensive; in fact, it is getting cheaper and cheaper to create increasingly advanced systems. The Web has made this possible because it is a free market for innovation, defined by a few qualities:

- Only good innovations succeed. Users are the only people who decide if something is valuable, so bad products are not rewarded.

Innovators (many of whom are individuals, not companies) are motivated by passion; after all, they had the idea in the first place. This usually means their work is better.

- Everyone with Internet access can learn how to program and can, within days, write a useful application and make it available to the whole world. No special permission is required.

Compare these qualities to government information technology:

- We buy software before our users can decide if it is valuable and user-friendly, meaning there's less incentive for developers to make a high-quality product.

- The programmers who develop our tools are under contract, and their responsibility is simply to fulfill their contract requirements. They often have little contact with the intended users, which keep them from understanding users' needs and preferences.

- It's near impossible for a new developer to enter the government contract market, leaving us a much smaller pool of software developers to work with.

That's not to say that our systems haven't come a long way in the last few years. We now have wikis, blogs, link sharing tools, and all the other basics associated with the "Web 2.0" brand. But we still rely on an outdated, inefficient system for procuring our software. Our systems have recently begun looking like the Web. Now it's time to start innovating like the Web, too. With recession-induced budget cuts on the way, it is the perfect time to justify a more cost-effective strategy. Here are three ways we can start.

Let analysts solve their own problems. Problems are best understood by those who experience them first hand. Many of the Web's best tools were not intended to be products; rather, their creators built them simply to solve their own problems. Basecamp, the Web's most popular project management tool, was created by a small Web development firm to help its remote staff collaborate. It proved so useful that the firm, 37Signals, quit creating Web sites and made the Basecamp suite its sole product. Basecamp is a good solution because its creators understand the problem the software solves. The same goes for the national security community. Intelligence officers understand their problems better than anyone. Ideally they would write their own software. But that's a tall order: few officers have the skills or the time for programming.

The solution is to hire Web programmers and embed them in analysis cells. By working as analysts, they'll understand our IT needs better than any outside contractor ever could. Give these developer-analysts the permission to write and deploy their own code, so that they may test various tools with their colleagues. Those colleagues would provide frequent, unfiltered feedback, a vital aspect of software development that is absent from the government procurement process.

Give independent Web developers a shot. Developer-analysts wouldn't be the only people with good ideas for new software. Small companies and independent developers have created thousands of Web-based productivity tools that would instantly help intelligence officers do their jobs better: To-do lists, journals, calendars, Gantt chart generators, people directories, mapping tools, timeline builders, concept mappers, and more.

But right now, most small companies and individuals can't compete for government contracts. Their products are too simple to justify the cost of the bidding process—not just for the developers, but probably for the government as well. Why spend several months acquiring something that takes only a few days to build? As a result, government networks don't benefit from the tools that make the Web so powerful.

We need to make opportunities for outside developers to get involved. For inspiration, look to Vivek Kundra, the Chief Technology Officer of the Washington, DC government. In an October 2008 contest called Apps For Democracy he procured 40 Web applications from dozens of solo developers and small firms. And he did it in 30 days on a $50,000 budget. He avoided the standard procurement route, which would have cost over $2 million and taken more than a year. Instead, he sponsored a contest that awarded small cash prizes to the best entries. Among the best tools were a carpool coordinator, a bike route mapper, and a neighborhood data visualizer.

The DC government probably never would have thought to request these tools, let alone issue RFPs for them. The entrants—DC residents and everyday programmers—had their own good ideas. Given the chance to realize them, they did.

The national security community should do the same thing. Thousands of Americans would respond with worthwhile contributions. Intelligence officers could team up with developers to help them better understand our needs. Officers with programming experience might even submit their own applications—a digital version of the DNI's Galileo Awards. In the end, we would have hundreds of tools at a very small cost. If the contest yielded just one useful application, the return on investment would be no less than that of the average mega-contract.

Open our eyes to Open Source Software. Even better than cheap software is free software. Many of the Web's best software is "open source," meaning anyone can download it at no cost. Most government networks are already running some open source products. Apache was created by volunteers and now powers over half of all Web servers, including Intelink. MediaWiki—the software that runs Wikipedia and Intellipedia—is also an open source project.

Open source software is useful because it is infinitely customizable. Anyone may modify an open source package to fit their precise needs. The government, on the other hand, too often reinvents the wheel: we pay exorbitant prices for proprietary tools when a few modifications to existing open source products would suffice. The FBI wasted over $200 million on SAIC's ultimately scrapped Virtual Case File, a content management system that would have done much the same thing as WordPress, the popular Weblogging software. In an attempt to fix the terrorist watch list, Lockheed Martin has spent $500 million on a database that cannot search for names. Anyone who has built a Web site with the open source MySQL database language knows what a shameful waste that is.

The Web is full of successful open source projects that would immediately prove useful to national security officers. Why aren't they more abundant on government networks?

Many believe that open source software poses a security risk because anyone may view and contribute to the code. This transparency actually makes the code more secure: for malicious code to make its way into an application, it would have to be approved by the project managers and evade the watchful eyes of hundreds of honest contributors. Should a user have any concerns about portions of the code, he may always remove them from his own copy. Proprietary code, on the other hand, can never be modified by the user.

In the long term, open source software is not completely without cost. It takes time and money to maintain. But the initial investment of simply trying it is minimal. While custom solutions can take years to complete, open source packages literally take minutes to deploy. Instead of seeing them as inferior alternatives, they should be the first place we look to fill our software needs. This is not likely to happen as long as managers lack guidance. So the first step is for agencies to adopt official policies that explicitly identify open source software as a preferred option.

The defense industry used to set the standard for information technology. The military was using the Internet and e-mail decades before the general public first heard of them. Today technology transfer works in reverse. New information tools are created by and for the public; bureaucracies catch on years later.

What can we learn from this? Should we try to get our edge back? No. It's not a bad thing that outsiders have gotten so good at software development. The only problem is our own refusal to adopt their superior innovation model, choosing instead to stick with our bureaucratic process. The Web's lesson for us is twofold:

Good software tools require lots of experimentation in order to find the sweet spot with users. Millions of dollars and months of planning for perfection are no replacement for simple trial and error.

Such experimentation has to be fast and low-cost. It cannot be weighed down by a bureaucratic contracting process.

Becoming comfortable with experimentation is the best thing you can do to prepare for any threat, and here's why: In order to be truly prepared, the available solutions must outnumber the problems. Otherwise, we'll have sunk our resources into a handful of tools that address some threats and ignore the rest. That is not preparation: it's gambling.

THE FUTURE OF CYBERSPACE SECURITY: THE LAW OF THE RODEO

BOB GOURLEY

Predictions of the future of technology are increasingly starting to sound like science fiction, with powerful computing grids giving incredible computational power to users and with autonomous robots becoming closer and closer to being in our daily lives vice just in computer science departments. Infotech, nanotech and biotech are fueling each other and each of those three dominate fields are generating more and more benefits that impact the other, propelling us even faster into a new world. Depending on your point of view the increasing pace of science and technology can be good or bad. As for me, I'm an optimist, and I know we humans will find a way to ensure technology serves our best interests.

But a sad fact of the human condition is that bad people will likely be with us long into the future. And sometimes good people can be tempted to do bad things, so we really need to engineer solutions that keep the bad guys from benefiting from technology and keep those who can sometimes be tempted from giving in to their darker side.

So is it possible to engineer perfectly secure systems? Consider the law of the rodeo: "There's not a horse that's never been rode, and not a rider that's never been thrown." I like the analogy since it reminds us that all computer evil can be mitigated. But it always fights back. Good and evil will continue a fast paced rodeo dance long into the future.

Our future growth, security and success as a nation depends in large part on a stable and secure information environment. To engineer secure systems that make up that environment we need to continually assess where we are technically and what the near term future holds for our technologies. Here are a few short predictions that could be useful in such a discussion:

Remote power is here today and will soon be widely distributed. This will allow small power consumption devices (like keyboards, mice, bluetooth headsets, hearing aides, small sensors) to be provided power by RF energy.

Power generation from motion is almost ready for prime time. This will allow devices to gain energy from vibrations, like the vibrations in a bridge when a car passes over it, or the vibrations in a wall of a building when the wind blows past it, or the vibrations caused by a person's movement through the day.

Communication capability (bandwidth) between fixed facilities will increase 1000 fold over the next five years. Cellular systems are on a dramatic improvement slope. My view: AT&T seems to lead in speed this year. Verizon will probably lead next year.

More users will be on the net. There are about 1.3 billion PC's connected to the Internet today. There are about 3.3 billion active cell phone subscriber accounts today. Those numbers will grow.

Storage, especially flash storage technologies, is decreasing in price so much we can afford to store data anywhere on almost anything.

Chips are being designed in ways that actually beat the old Moore's Law projections. This is being done by placing many cores on one chip. Very high data rate capabilities are being connected directly to the cores on these chips.

RFID is becoming so widespread we can place devices on everything that allows devices to report back what they are and what they are for and where they have been.

All this capabilities are being networked together, including increasingly direct device-to-device connections via capabilities provided by enhanced protocols (especially IPv6).

Consumer devices, especially consumer communication devices, are becoming increasingly capable. What used to be called a cell phone is now a phone, video recorder, video editor, entertainment, and mobile office device with location aware data (GPS).

Social networking sites/tools such as Facebook will expand till one day 100% of the population will have active, up to date, authoritative online profiles.

There are many other elements of the future relevant to security discussions, but the projections above lead to some interesting conclusions on their own. Lets think through some of the impacts of the givens above:

Bad actors who want to exploit systems will increasingly not have to worry about them being powered off. They will be on all the time.

Bad actors will increasingly be able to exploit social systems to gather data pre-attack. However, the powerful trust models of social networks may offer a counter to some of these attacks.

Many paths into devices will be available for unauthorized users to exploit. And if they are compromised by people or code that intend on generating denial of service attacks, huge amounts of bandwidth will exist for them to attack from.

When a bad actor gets through defenses into data stores, they will likely find a wide range of data to exploit, since it is becoming so easy and low cost for us to store everything.

Having things networked together means it can be easier to penetrate a target by finding one weak link that is connected to the infrastructure.

Areas of people's lives they once thought private, especially their cell phones and the data on their cell phones, are increasingly becoming attractive targets to hackers.

What sort of security regime is needed in an environment like the one portrayed above? I am a career technologist and considered by some to be an information security expert, but neither I nor any of my peers can pretend to know that there are perfect solutions for these problems. Some solutions I think would receive universal support:

- Enhanced firewalls and intrusion detection devices to stop the readily stoppable.

- More ready and granular configuration control, for all devices. When a device is out of configuration it must be brought back into compliance immediately.

- Better laws and treaties concerning cyberspace. Deterrence policies by governments, for example.

- More attention to standards and to industry organizations (including supply chain quality organizations) is a must.

- Better training and education for all (I mean ALL) humans connected to the grid.

- Better, continuously adaptive anti-virus solutions.

- Automated attack response (not counterattack, response).

- Enhanced, easier to use encryption.

- Enhanced, more secure and easy to use identity and authorization technologies.

- Insider threat modeling and analysis which can be integrated into all technologies.

Information technology (IT) is the enabler for nearly every endeavor in the modern world. Our economy, healthcare, food supply and national security are dependent on IT. The intellectual property of our nation's academic and corporate thinkers is held within IT. Global finance is conducted with IT. All indications are that our dependencies on IT will only increase, but we have yet to see an equally rapid or significant advance in the realm of IT security. Cyber defenders, law enforcement professionals, systems engineers and computer security experts work around the clock to help protect our IT enterprises, but at present we are fighting a losing battle. With "change" on the agenda we are at a critical decision point. Continuing to track along the present trend lines leaves us less secure—and our world less stable—by the day. Taking decisive and disruptive action will put our adversaries on the defensive and help ensure that the future that IT enables is one that promulgates knowledge and wealth globally.

SECURITY EVOLUTION

GUNNAR PETERSON

We have been in a world of faith-based security for far too long. Probably the most important cause is a lack of innovation and dynamism in the discipline of information security. Consider the following rough timeline of software development progress since the dawn of the web.

People pretty quickly realized that plain HTML was not enough, so developers invented CGI/PERL for more dynamic sites. Once they wanted to scale and pool they built out ASP and JSP, then to deliver middle tier components they developed EJB, J2EE, and DCOM. After that there were a lot of heterogeneous systems that needed to talk to each other so SOAP and XML came along to address that. This path diverged into ultra-simple (REST) and more powerful but baroque (SOA), and finally, the user side got some love with Web 2.0 technologies. That's a heck of a lot of engineering and innovation by the software development community for plus or minus 8 years.

Now lets' check in with the developers' brethren over in information security (INFOSEC). Well, once the web came along the information security community quickly realized that network address translation was going to be important, and further that encrypting the communication channel between the browser and the web server was also crucial. And then, they addressed all the security issues ASP, JSP, EJB, J2EE, DCOM, SOAP, XML, REST, SOA, and Web 2.0 with....umm...more of the same!

	Developers	Security
1995	CGI, PERL	Network firewalls, SSL
1997	ASP, JSP	Network firewalls, SSL
1998	EJB, J2EE, DCOM	Network firewalls, SSL
1999	SOAP, XML	Network firewalls, SSL
2001	Rest, SOA	Network firewalls, SSL
2003	Web 2.0	Network firewalls, SSL

Figure 3. Growth of development technologies v. growth of security technologies. (Illustration by Gunnar Peterson)

That's a pretty poor showing for innovation considering the enterprise investment into information security. Sure the software developers' have a bigger budget, but come on INFOSEC—show some pride!

INFOSEC types like to throw developers under the bus for security issues, but it's a collective failure. Sure developers need to learn more about secure coding, but as the table above shows - security is not keeping pace, and the gap is getting bigger.

Here is another dimension to the problem—attackers *do* evolve. The new technologies provide far greater attack surface (data, method and channels) for the attackers to exploit and/or launch attacks from.

Because the defenses have not evolved, it's a simple evolutionary adaptation for attackers to go around or through the 1995 defenses. It's not about SOAP going through the firewall, its about never bothering to secure the apps and the data. Its like saying to your opponent, remember the how the Detroit Lions played defense in a certain game in 1995, we were just going to do that.

Attackers exploit new functionality & data

	Developers	Security
1995	CGI, PERL	Network firewalls, SSL
1997	ASP, JSP	Network firewalls, SSL
1998	EJB, J2EE, DCOM	Network firewalls, SSL
1999	SOAP, XML	Network firewalls, SSL
2001	Rest, SOA	Network firewalls, SSL
2003	Web 2.0	Network firewalls, SSL

Tunnel in/around/under archaic defenses

Figure 4. Attack strategies versus non-evolving security strategies. (Illustration by Gunnar Peterson)

So with the software developer's latest evolution we get Mr. O'Reilly's famous Web 2.0 meme map:

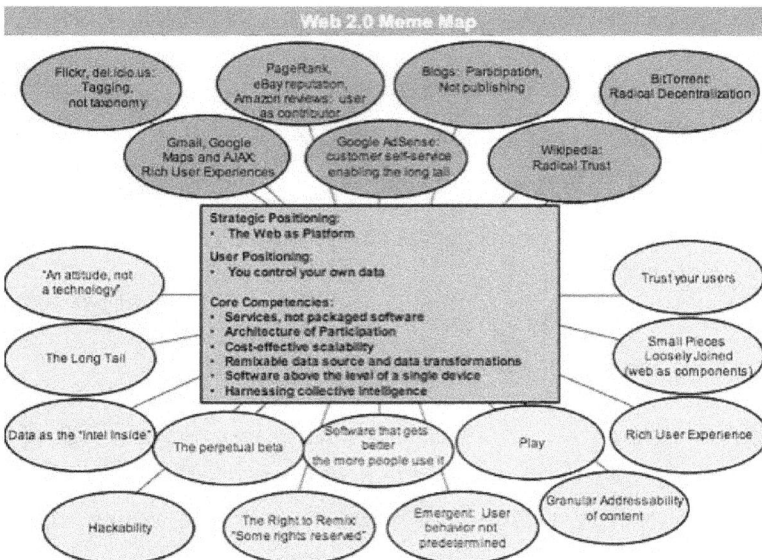

Figure 5. O'Reilly Web 2.0 meme map. (Illustration by O'Reilly Publishing)

But where is the co-evolution in INFOSEC? There is none. There is co-evolution in the attacker space. Here is a sample web 2.0 attacker meme map:

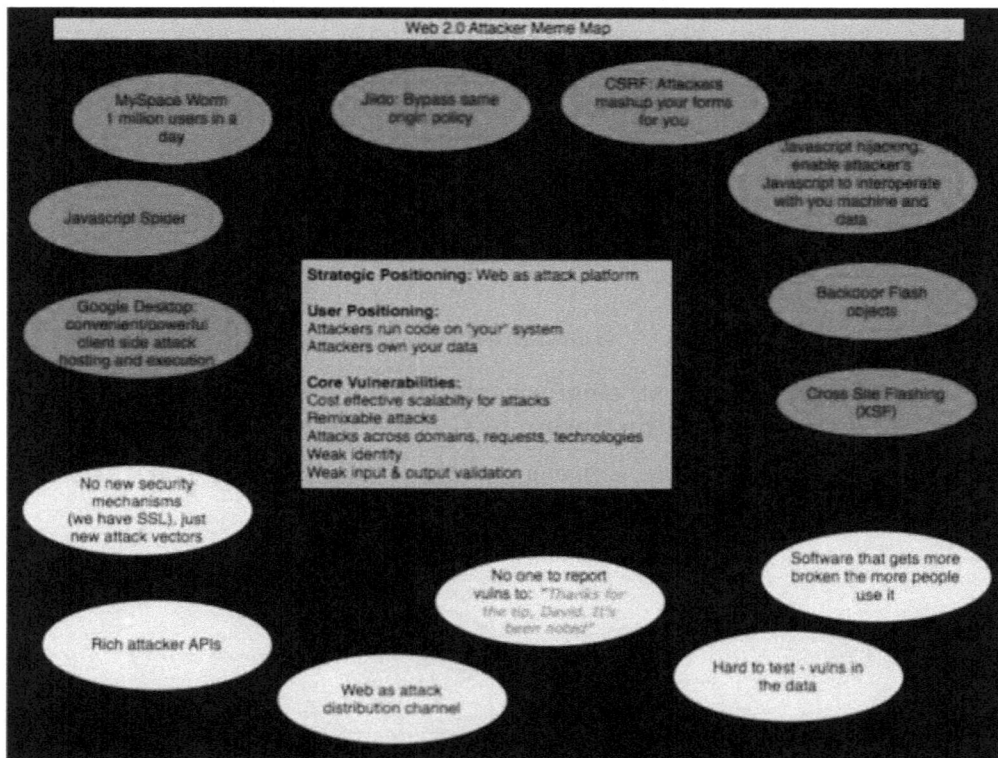

Figure 6. Attacker meme map. (Illustration by Gunnar Peterson)

So the firewall offers great protection if your adversary is using Visio, but otherwise it's mostly useless.

So we would want to see two things happen—developers start writing more high assurance code and second—INFOSEC needs to evolve its security services to form fit to that which they are protecting. Hint: it ain't a Visio diagram.

Rich functionality & data

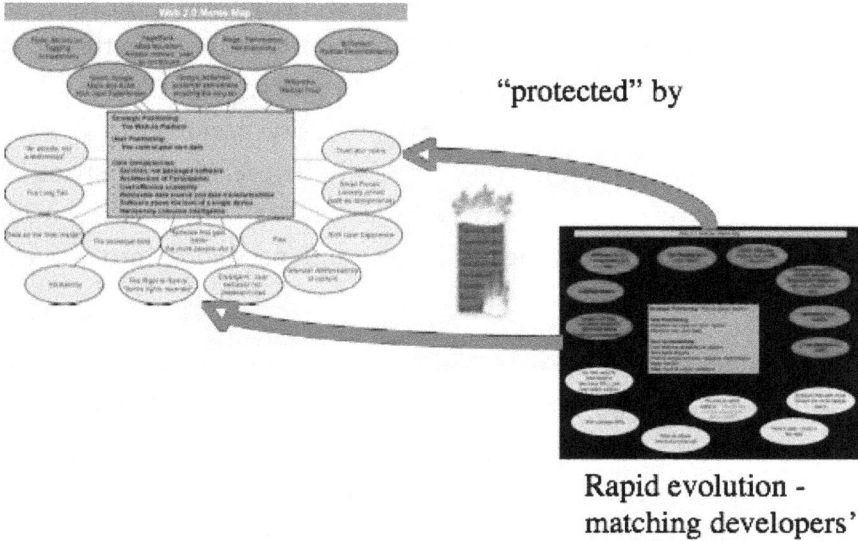

"protected" by

Rapid evolution -
matching developers'

**Figure 7. Rapidly evolving security strategies.
(Illustrations by Gunnar Peterson and O'Reilly
Publishing)**

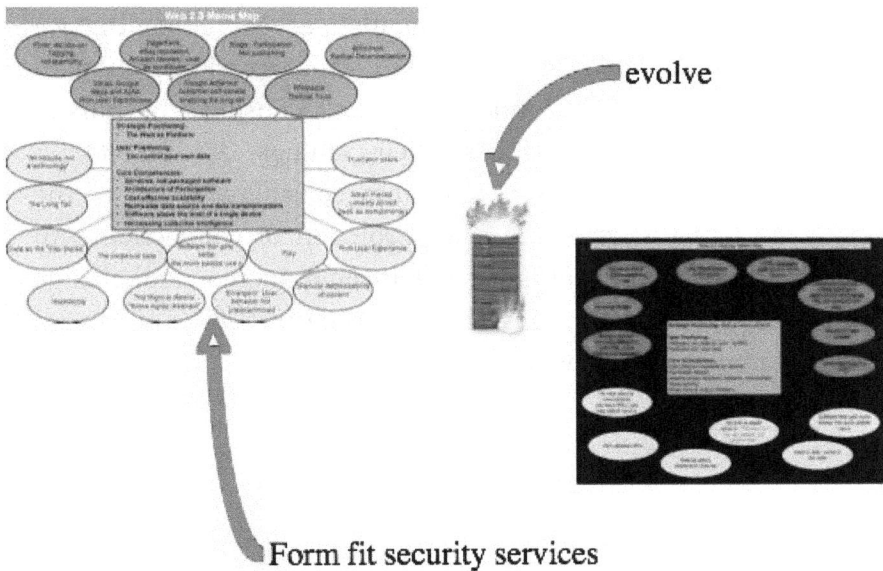

evolve

Form fit security services

**Figure 8. Form-fitting security services. (Illustrations
by Gunnar Peterson and O'Reilly Publishing)**

The thing is—we are getting better tools. Static analysis is a very powerful tool to improve your software security from a bottom up perspective and it can scale. These tools continue to get better. We are getting better standards—WS-Security, WS-Trust, and company enable fundamentally new security architectures. And we're getting better primitives, especially in the identity space—SAML, Cardspace, and friends will one day let us live in a world where users are not typing username and password into a web browser to do online banking.

So maybe the innovation tide is turning, but there is a lot of ground to catch up. INFOSEC is about a decade behind the developers and probably close to that far behind the attackers. It's going to take something special if not dramatic to catch up, The status quo will not do if we hope to see truly secure systems in our lifetime. Catching up is going to require that we stop thinking of security architecture problems as easily drawn and manipulated diagrams and remembering that diagrams represent things that are real, many of which are not readily manipulated. More than that we need to remember that systems are used – and occasionally abused – by people; technical solutions that don't consider the human factor are all around us and their failings are legend. A comprehensive security effort takes into consideration all of the factors impacting a system, not just protocols or connections. An effective security effort will not come through incremental change but through *evolutionary* leaps whose wisdom and effectiveness are demonstrated in the real world.

ARMING FOR THE SECOND WAR OF IDEAS

MATT ARMSTRONG

> *As a nation, everything we do and everything we fail to say or do will have its impact in other lands. – Presidential candidate Dwight D. Eisenhower, 1952*

Today, perceptions created and forged by words and deeds, some of which may be violent acts, are part of orchestrated efforts to gain strategic influence over friends, foes, and neutrals. The importance of speaking directly to people to support national security objectives has been elemental in world affairs since World War II. However, with détente in the latter half of the Cold War, the value and purpose was lost.

The collapse of the Soviet Union and the end of superpower politics shaped by "traditional" diplomacy plus the rise of the Internet and New Media combined to return the power to the people, so to speak. America's adversaries have quickly adapted to the new environment using information as force multipliers. Today, bullets and bombs often have a much smaller impact than the propaganda opportunities they create – opportunities to influence public opinion and build public support.

When there are no capitals to take or "hearts" to be "won", real security comes through enduring engagement of local and global groups in a modern proxy struggle for minds and wills. The nature of informational engagement places less emphasis on direct engagement and more on indirect engagement. This force multiplier effect relies on operating by, with, and through people who are local to the target audiences. In the Internet Age when physical distances are virtually eliminated, this "locality" does not have to be physical; it can be cultural, political, or social. Writing to Abu Musab al-Zarqawi in 2005, Ayman al-Zawahiri stated that "we are in a battle, and that more than half of this battle is taking place in the battlefield of the media [*sic*]."[131]

While the U.S. has come around to the importance of public opinion, forward progress is, at best, slow. Policymakers and legislators continue to debate the role of persuasion through means other than brute force to national security imperatives from economics, health, terrorism, and war. Our adversaries, however, are moving ahead and increasingly using the tools and techniques developed within the United States.

In 2008, the dean of international relations at the Russian foreign ministry's Diplomatic Academy said:

> *"The Russian government must prepare to fight information wars which are becoming an ever more important part of geopolitical life, restoring parts of the Soviet-era system and going beyond that as well..."*[132]

The Chinese meanwhile are spending time exploring "informatized warfare," "attitude warfare," and "perception warfare" as modern application of Sun Tzu's famous if oft-forgotten dictum of defeating an enemy without fighting. A book by two Chinese colonels also reminds us that the real battlespace today is far broader than two sides firing bullets at each other.[133]

In 2001, Richard Holbrooke asked how "can a man in a cave out-communicate the world's leading communications society?" Answering his own question, he suggested the cause was the

[131] Ayman al-Zawahiri, "Zawahiri's Letter to Zarqawi " (Countering Terrorism Center's Harmony Document Database, 2005).
[132] From http://windowoneurasia.blogspot.com/2008/10/window-on-eurasia-moscow-must-gear-up.html
[133] Qiao Liang and Wang Xiangsui, "Unrestricted Warfare." (Beijing, PLA Literature and Arts Publishing House, 1999),
http://mountainrunner.us/library/uw/unrestricted_warfare.html.

"apparent initial failure of our own message and the inadequacy of our messengers."[134] But how is it that in 2009, the Secretary of Defense continues to ask the same question with the same indictment?[135]

An obscure group in 1998, Al-Qaeda achieved global prominence and influence with mutually reinforcing words, images, and actions. The United States responded with showcases of Americana that, not surprisingly, failed to resonate with the target audiences: our enemies' base, moderates, "swing voters", and even our friends and allies. Perhaps most importantly, the U.S. ignored the link between policy and the psychological impact of information to persuade and dissuade American public diplomacy and strategic communication became an irrelevant whisper and "beauty contest" in stark contrast to the adversary's active propaganda of words and deeds. In the "war of ideas," the United States was largely unaware and unarmed and accordingly lost influence and stature, increasing vulnerabilities not only in the military domain, but in economic, financial, and diplomatic realms too.

In 2009, the U.S. government has become more aware and effective of the information realm but understanding the need and means of global engagement remains elusive. Point solutions continue to come out of Congress and think tanks and while some have traction few if any recognize the need for establishing principles and to properly arm for what is many respects a Second War of Ideas. The most significant impediment to acknowledging and arming for the new reality is the forgotten memory of the First War of Ideas.

---

[134] Richard Holbrooke, "Get the Message Out," *The Washington Post*, October 28 2001.
[135] Robert M. Gates, "A Balanced Strategy: Reprogramming the Pentagon for a New Age," *Foreign Affairs* 88, no. 1 (2009).

Even classic *realpolitik* authors like E.H. Carr and Hans Morgenthau understood the importance of public opinion, information and perceptions. In his seminal <u>Twenty Years Crisis</u>, E.H. Carr described the rise of the "power over opinion" as "the morale of the civilian population became for the first time a military objective."[136] Morgenthau, writing in <u>Politics Among Nations</u>, listed nine components of national power and described two as unstable caused by informational that would today be called "soft power."[137]

Even George Kennan's Theory of Containment was based not on the force of arms but on the force of ideas. Diplomacy had "almost no place in containment policy that emerged after 1945" as the Russians were considered fanatics. They were an ideological threat, not a normal geopolitical threat.[138]

The U.S. knew the Russians were unable and unwilling to enter into another hot war. They did not need to for the very simple reason that subversion was far cheaper. The "war of ideology" was very real. United States Ambassador to Russia said the most important "fact in the field of foreign policy today...is the fact the Russians have declared psychological war on the United States, all over the world." It was, he continued, "a war of ideology and a fight unto the death."[139] The struggle for authority and relevance was not in the arena of power but the arena of ideas and international persuasion.

---

[136] Edward Hallett Carr, *The Twenty Years' Crisis: 1919-1939* (London,: Macmillan & co. ltd, 1946), 136.

[137] Hans J. Morgenthau and Kenneth W. Thompson, *Politics among Nations: The Struggle for Power and Peace*, 6th ed. (New York: Knopf: Distributed by Random House, 1985). See esp. Ch. 9.

[138] Richard Lock-Pullan in Andrew M. Dorman and Greg Kennedy, eds., *War & Diplomacy: From World War I to the War on Terrorism* (Washington, D.C.: Potomac Books,2008), 104.

[139] Frank A. Ninkovich, *The Diplomacy of Ideas: U.S. Foreign Policy and Cultural Relations, 1938-1950* (Cambridge [Eng.]; New York: Cambridge University Press, 1981), 135.

It was essential for the U.S. to become capable in this realm. It was also financially prudent. In the words of General Electric's chairman who testified in support of the Smith-Mundt Bill in 1947, that it would "do more to reduce the risk of war, and thus to reduce the need for a multibillion dollar military force, than any other single factor."[140]

Today, the "war of ideas" is admittedly problematic. The phrase suggests there is an end with two possibilities: win or lose. It also suggests a known adversary. Both were more fitting of the struggle in the Cold War but today not only are the threats far more diverse, but the mobilizing effect has been diluted by overuse in domestic politics with phrases like the "war on drugs," "war on crime," and the "war on poverty."

The U.S. must, however, continue to prepare as if it is arming for a Second War of Ideas. This means reviewing past practices. Arming for the First War of Ideas included passing the Smith-Mundt Act, officially known as Public Law 402: the United States Information and Educational Exchange Act of 1948. The anchor for nearly all of America's global engagement then and today, it passed with bipartisan support in the House and Senate – with opposition primarily from the Midwest – and was signed into law by President Harry S. Truman on January 27, 1948. It was a collaborative effort by the State Department and Congress with significant and broad support from the media and academia.

On the eve of its passage, the nascent National Security Council recognized the broad threat to America's security and directed the State Department to respond to the "coordinated psychological,

---

[140] Shawn J. Parry-Giles, *The Rhetorical Presidency, Propaganda, and the Cold War, 1945-1955*, Praeger Series in Presidential Studies, (Westport, Conn.: Praeger, 2002), 14.

political and economic measures designed to undermine non-Communist elements in all countries."[141]

Today, the U.S. must expand its horizon and realize there are more adversaries than "violent extremists," "Islamists", or other derivative labels for Al-Qaeda, Taliban, and associated movements from the Middle East to South Asia. Narrowly defining America's adversaries is myopic and dangerous.

We need an effective and flexible arsenal of persuasion in the global information environment and global economic environment that goes beyond ideological support for terrorism and insurgency and into protecting broader interests, from the economy to global health to reconstruction and stabilization efforts. The new arsenal of persuasion must be adept against all adversaries in the entire global information environment.

To build this arsenal, the U.S. requires leadership, principles, purpose, and collaboration between Congress and the Administration. It is noteworthy that in 2008, Secretary of Defense Robert M. Gates, as well as the Chairman of the Joint Chiefs of Staff, Michael Mullen, were both very vocal on rebuilding public diplomacy. As the Bush Administration wound down at the end of 2008, reports from think tanks (and government agencies) recommending change in how the U.S. engages in the world became more numerous. Whether this engagement was called public diplomacy or strategic communication, or both, one characteristic was shared by nearly every report: a nearly complete absence of support by Secretary of State Condoleezza Rice. President George W. Bush's fourth Under Secretary of State for Public Diplomacy and Public Affairs, James K. Glassman, was vocal, visible, and active in resurrecting the primacy of the State

---

[141] Nicholas J. Cull, *The Cold War and the United States Information Agency: American Propaganda and Public Diplomacy, 1945-1989* (Cambridge University Press, 2008), 39.

Department and public diplomacy, but with little to no visible support from his boss, or his bosses boss, only so much could be achieved. Calls to simply throw more money to the State Department ignore the realities of Congressional mandates and, more importantly, confidence. Glassman himself would not begin asking for more money until the end of his brief tenure because he knew substantial change was a required prerequisite to both asking for and using new money.

The principle function of public diplomacy is the direct or indirect engagement of foreign publics to support national security objectives. It operates by, with, and through indigenous speakers to enhance credibility and the peer awareness. Public diplomacy is primarily about creating discourse more along the lines of "them versus them" and less about comparing the U.S. to a third party. To focus on the latter encourages the "beauty contest" mentality of since 9/11 and reinforces the need to ask the question, "Why do they hate us?"

The Internet and global travel have diffused and made public opinion more important. Global connectivity has virtually eliminated the distance between two points and at the same time radically increased the diversity of the audience for any issue. The product of this change is a challenge to the traditional concepts of nationalism, power, and state autonomy. New "imagined communities" transcending geo-political borders mean the essence and even utility of nationalism and state loyalty must be reconsidered as engagement must be simultaneously local, global, individual and collective.

It is misleading and even naïve to suggest that today the mere access to information is a catalyst for action. Information by itself does not create action or shape perceptions. Alone, information by itself is meaningless. It must have context to make it resonate with the target audience. It is one thing to hear about death and oppression in another country, but without a perceived stake in or connection to an event, as well as an ability to influence future events, the knowledge has little meaning.

Actions reinforce words, which are reinforced by repetition, and narratives from a person or collective histories all give meaning to the information or to make the information meaningless. The "global village" in which people share values and beliefs far outside the traditional geo-political administrative units of the past, otherwise known as nation-states, means connections between people may be virtual and actions are motivated by empathy. What is local can also be global just as global is the new local. Being "local" to a conflict is not simply a characteristic of geography but of socio-cultural frameworks that invoke a new kind of stateless nationalism and empathy. This is a key battleground of the mind as efforts must be managed and supported in new ways.

The purpose of global engagement is not to make people love America, as the phrase "winning hearts and minds" suggests. The U.S. is in a constant and enduring struggle for the minds and wills of people around the globe. This struggle does not take place in a bifurcated environment where the U.S. is a detached and sterile environment from the rest of the global informational ecosystem. Global perceptions are shaped by what happens inside America's borders. This struggle does not take place in a "clean room" beyond America's borders that does not and must not "taint" sensitive American eyes and ears, but in a global environment. What is said and done in the U.S. has worldwide reach because ideas are not confined by geo-political borders, including our own. Myopic and temporally challenged visions of who the enemy is and will be and where and how the struggle takes place must be updated by the principles and purpose of a global, not simply "international" or "overseas," engagement. Perhaps the simplest example is Latin America: to communicate to South and Central America, one need only broadcast in Spanish within the United States.

Targeting the "hearts" of people may feel good, but likability is not necessary. Action is necessary. The ability to influence what people do is essential. The action can be active or passive. Providing direct support to an American national security objective can be just as important as denying support to activities that are against our national security. Support can be material, like money, shelter, or equipment. It can also be moral, social, and political.

President Harry S. Truman invoked the struggle and President Dwight D. Eisenhower made the struggle part of his foreign policy plank speech as candidate a central focus of his national security strategy. In fact, he went further and admitted the truth about the struggle: "Don't be afraid of that term just because it's a five-dollar, five syllable word... Psychological warfare is the struggle for minds and wills of men."[142] Addressing public opinion was essential then and it is essential today.

Success is not found in answering the question "why do they hate us" or in "winning hearts", but in understanding and correcting the conditions and perceptions that permit and even encourage extremism, insurgency, and terrorism to take hold and propagate.

The psychological struggle of the Cold War is lost by those who remember only the military confrontation. The "predominant aspect of the new diplomacy," wrote a young Henry Kissinger, "is its psychological dimension." [143] But by the late 1960's, as the borders of the most important contested spaces were settled, the strategic value of this "new diplomacy" gave way to private, closed door diplomacy. The result was the transformation of what is now known as public diplomacy from a national security imperative

---

[142] Kenneth Alan Osgood, *Total Cold War: Eisenhower's Secret Propaganda Battle at Home and Abroad* (Lawrence: University of Kansas, 2006), 46.
[143] Ibid., 182.

aggressively targeting foreign public opinion to something more resembling a passive "beauty contest."

It is important to realize that the global nature of the struggle began to die with détente. The utility of inoculating or agitating foreign publics diminished. In fact, the strategic value of public diplomacy was troublesome and interfering with closed door diplomacy. By the collapse of the Soviet Union, Congress only knew the "hard power" options and jumped at the chance to dump the tools of international engagement that had no perceptible value.

Symbolic of this shift was Senator J. William Fulbright's attack on the United States Information Agency and international broadcasting in the early 1970s. The marginalization of public opinion in the face of Great Power politics was clear when he said that America's "Radios [Voice of America, Radio Free Europe, and Radio Liberty] should be given an opportunity to take their rightful place in the graveyard of Cold War relics."[144] After a New York Senator showed a USIA film on his monthly statewide television show for his constituents, Fulbright claimed the screening violated the Smith-Mundt Act. Acting U.S. Attorney General Richard Kleindienst demurred, saying the language and "apparent purpose" of the section that prohibited the State Department from domestic dissemination "was to make USIA materials available to the American public through the press and members of Congress."[145] The Senator spent the last of his political capital for an amendment

---

[144] Cull, *The Cold War and the United States Information Agency: American Propaganda and Public Diplomacy, 1945-1989*, 314-15. An "anti-Fulbright faction" would develop against the Chairman of the Foreign Relations Committee that was likely the product of the Nixon Administration in response to his attacks on the USIA. It got so bad that Fulbright would demurred sponsoring legislation the State Department asked for, saying "Why should I offer it? It will just be beaten." See John Finney, "Vote in Senate Gives Fulbright Another in a Series of Rebuffs," *New York Times*, May 26 1972.
[145] John W. Finney, "Kleindienst Says Buckley Can Show U.S.I.A.'S Film," *New York Times*, April 1 1972.

to close what he saw as a "loophole." Previously, the Act stated that material "shall be available" to the media, academia, the public, and Congress. Now the Act read that "any such information shall not be disseminated within the United States."[146] The Foreign Relations Act of 1972 changed the clause on distribution.

This is neither insignificant nor trivial. It means the American public, Congress, and much of the rest of the Government is cut off from what happens overseas in America's name. The transparency intended by Congress six decades ago is now opacity with little in the way of democratic oversight, or insight, into the global activities of the Government. This bifurcation of a U.S. and non-U.S. information sphere is artificial, uniquely American, quaint, and ultimately not based on Congressional intent in 1948 or modern requirements. This veil must be lifted.

Sixty years after the Act was passed, rumor and disinformation play an even greater role in today's 24/7 global information environment. First impressions matter more than ever and perceptions make or break confidence in everything from financial markets to issues of global health. As the U.S. media retreats from overseas coverage and news bureaus shrink, the wealth of information available today is surpassed only by the poverty of attention by both the media and consumer.

Dramatic and sometimes tectonic changes are required to adapt to the modern environment. It is essential to accept that we are in a global information environment. The world's information eco-systems are alive and vibrant and have little in common with geo-political borders, especially those of the United States. This means returning transparency into the overseas conversations and actions by the Government. It also means competition with U.S. news bureaus. In 1947, the backers of the Smith-Mundt Bill repeatedly

---

[146] Sec. 204 of the Foreign Relations Act of 1972 (P.L. 92-352)

made clear the purpose of the government news service was to reach where the American media could not. Attempts to privatize the whole program were rebuffed by the media as too expensive but written in the Act were requirements to use private resources wherever possible. The Marshall Plan, the greatest foreign aid program the U.S. ever conducted, expanded the support for private resources even further.[147] The increased awareness of Governmental activities beyond the borders will create constituencies for successful programs and punish poor policies and deception.

This is reinforced by an institutional culture that fosters the firewalling of active engagement done overseas from the passive engagement done within the U.S. which leds to the erroneous belief that public affairs should "inform without influence."[148] If the neutral delivery of information to the American public was truly a driving concern, neither Administration officials nor Congress should be permitted on the Sunday Talk Show circuit and elections should be dramatically shortened with strict controls on political advertising and speech.

A former Assistant Secretary of State wrote in 1953 that "in the contest for men's minds, truth can be peculiarly the American weapon."[149] The same is true today. Influence need not be deceptive. A public affairs officer working on a military base in Middle America is exercising influence by informing the community that, say, a gate will be closed for repairs. The base commander would surely not waste his time connecting with the

---

[147] For more details on hearings to privatize Government broadcasting and the symbiotic relationship of the Marshall Plan and the Smith-Mundt Act, see Matt Armstrong, "Rethinking Smith-Mundt", http://mountainrunner.us/smith-mundt/.
[148] This phrase, and others very similar, was often raised to by public affairs officers, almost exclusively in the Defense Community.
[149] Edward Barrett quoted in Leo Bogart and Agnes Bogart, *Premises for Propaganda: The United States Information Agency's Operating Assumptions in the Cold War* (New York: Free Press, 1976), xv.

local population if he is not concerned with being a good "neighbor" or giving respect to the local population.

Further, public affairs officers (PAO) are presently trained in journalism and public relations. Modern public affairs personnel must be adept not at reactive engagement in which the method of communication is dictated, but pro-active, multi-modal engagement. The PAO for General Petraeus should not be a journalist by training, but must be well-versed in public diplomacy and international relations.

To better imagine the need for reform, the Smith-Mundt Act institutionalized a capability to directly address non-state actors. Abolishing the United States Information Agency in 1999 effectively abolished America's ability to effectively engage publics and even acknowledge the importance of non-state actors. A June 2008 report on the contemporary public diplomacy efforts noted that "there is no one overseas whose primary job responsibility is to interface with foreign audiences."[150]

The State Department has been unable to adapt to the twenty-first century (or even the twentieth considering the need to create the USIA). Effectively engaging in the Second War of Ideas requires creating a Department of Non-State, functionally if not bureaucratically, armed with the appropriate tools and comprehensive collaboration across agencies and countries and organizations. This entity must remain within the State Department lest the State Department becomes totally ignorant of the penetrating effects of public diplomacy in "traditional" diplomacy.

To better respond to present and future challenges, the State Department must be reorganized to match the regional

---

[150] http://mountainrunner.us/2008/06/from_the_us_advisory_commissio.html

requirements of the twenty-first century. This means operating at more macro level than individual countries. The regional bureaus must be given more power and re-aligned to match the Defense Department's Combatant Commands. A "super ambassador" at the head of each bureau would have resources that better correspond to the international requirements, to collaborate better with partners like the Defense Department, reduce the emphasis on countries, and more importantly put more power into the State Department.

All of these changes require substantial partnering with Congress. They also require leadership and support from the President on down. They are also required for America's national security.

Through the last thirty to forty years, the concepts of persuasion, influence, and even public diplomacy have become dirty words on par with "propaganda." How can it be that bullets and bombs can be valid tools of persuasion while information to persuade carries a stigma? Is it really better to kill an adversary rather than to directly or indirectly persuade him by the conveyance of truth and dispelling false rumors? Is it possible to bomb our adversaries into liking us? Surely the U.S. can better use information in a way that is not opposed to our democratic foundations in a way the 80th Congress found possible sixty years ago when it passed the Smith-Mundt Act to prevent, shorten, or terminate conflict today?

America's failure to understand or to participate in the war over public perception is not a noble act, but one of implicit suicide. Insurgents can now measure their success in terms of money, supplies, safe houses, and recruits—all of which come at the expense of trust in the United States and its influence on the people.

BLURRING THE LINES BETWEEN WAR AND PEACE

SHANE DEICHMAN

The evolution of conflict correlates with both political and technological inflection points in history. For instance, the political model of the modern nation-state—and its concomitant authority over a professional cadre of armed forces—traces its lineage to the Peace of Westphalia in 1648. That inflection point contained the religious violence that followed the Reformation and created both a new political order, and a new model of raising and sustaining armed forces.

Similarly, the dual popular revolutions in America and France at the end of the 18th century further refined the political model—and, under France's *levée en masse*, wove conventional military force structure into the fabric of society. The early 19th century saw massive mobilizations, with armies numbering over 100,000 clashing over wide swaths of land. Every facet of society became engaged in security:

> *The young men shall fight; the married men shall forge arms and transport provisions; the women shall make tents and clothes and shall serve in the hospitals; the children shall turn linen into lint; the old men shall betake themselves to the public squares in order to arouse the courage of the warriors and preach hatred of kings and the unity of the Republic.*[151]

The technical innovations of the industrial revolution provided dramatic increases in lethality. The rifled bore, indirect-fire artillery, aerial observation, and enhanced yield explosives led to

---

[151] *Levée en masse* as decreed by the French "National Convention" on 23 August 1793.

"massed fire" tactics and a tremendous increase in casualties (e.g., the Battle of Verdun in World War I, where more than a quarter million perished).

Mobility offered an antidote. The internal combustion engine coupled with wireless communications enabled "maneuver warfare," allowing forces to avoid direct confrontation with massed enemy forces in pursuit of economic and political targets. The ability to directly threaten the cultural and social elements of a nation-state, with devastating effect through nuclear weapons, led the great powers to a Cold War where proxy states bore the brunt of clashes.

CONTEXT OF MODERN CONFLICT

The events of September 11th, 2001 created another historical inflection point. While al Qaeda had been conducting hostile actions against the United States for years (*q.v.* the February 1993 World Trade Center bombing), 9/11 forced a global change in perspective. While the Cold War was defined by the meta-strategy of "Containment", the vernacular of security policy and force structure had not changed appreciably since that "other" 9/11: the 9 November 1989 fall of the Berlin Wall. Al Qaeda's successful attack on September 11th, 2001 served to underscore the inadequacy of our national security institutions, not only in countering threats but in even *acknowledging* them.

Since 2001, a number of theorists have filled this void in our strategic vernacular (notably Thomas P.M. Barnett, John Nagl and John Robb). Rather than supplant the logic of Karl von Clausewitz's "trinity" of *Rationality (political leadership), Probability (military leadership)* and *Popular Rage (the citizenry)*, our previous bias that placed undue primacy on political leadership has shifted toward the citizenry. The recently published *Field Manual 3-24/Marine Corps Warfighting Publication 3-33.5: Counterinsurgency* and *Field Manuel*

3-07: Stability Operations have further established "soft power" in the doctrinal foundation of the U.S. military.

Though the preponderance of U.S.-led expeditionary operations this decade have been in ostensibly "tribal clashes," representative of the shift in emphasis away from political leadership to the citizenry, the mechanisms of national power in the United States continue to emphasize the large-scale conventional threat as well as the small wars..[152] The failure of governmental institutions to effectively collaborate, while not surprising given its breadth and diversity, should be a top priority of Gen.(ret) Jones as he becomes President Obama's National Security Advisor and day-to-day leader of the National Security Council—the principal forum of the President for considering national security and foreign policy matters.

AMBIGUITY OF THREATS

The disproportionate investment by the United States in its security institutions (nearly equaling the combined military spending of the rest of the world[153]) has created a powerful deterrent to conventional military operations by other states. The quick eviction of Iraqi forces from Kuwait in 1991, the crumbling of the Taliban in Afghanistan in 2001, and the successful regime change in Iraq in 2003 all demonstrated the futility of challenging western (read "U.S.") military forces in open combat.

A logical by-product of such profound conventional superiority is for forces to disperse themselves, to adopt "guerilla-style" or asymmetric tactics, and to mask their forces within the very fabric

---

[152] Compare COL Gian Gentile's "Let's Build an Army to Win All Wars" with LTC(ret) John Nagl's *"Let's Win the Wars We're In"*, Joint Forces Quarterly, January 2009 (reprinted at http://smallwarsjournal.com/blog/2008/11/jfq-point-counterpoint-swj-ear/)

[153] SIPRI Yearbook 2008, Stockholm International Peace Research Institute, http://yearbook2008.sipri.org/ .

of civil society. The survival mechanisms afforded by such "cultural cloaking," while constraining force capabilities in terms of power projection, prove especially effective in local defense as well as in harassing operations.

The modern information revolution has spurred technical egalitarianism between national and sub-national forces. Where over-the-horizon communications were once the sole purview of national institutions, today even the most modest of organizations has a world-wide (and world-class) command and control architecture readily available. Furthermore, the proliferation of "do-it-yourself" (DIY) munitions has spread into the realm of artillery and rockets[154], and is only lacking guided thrust to create DIY cruise missiles.

These ambiguities create a dilemma for conventional military forces raised under the auspices of the Geneva Conventions. While central authority and "unity of command" are revered as core principles in nation-state based security institutions, they are anathema to asymmetric threats. In addition to resolving security concerns and communications challenges, decentralization also enhances adaptability of subordinate forces.

CONSEQUENCES

Institutions that adapt to exploit emerging opportunities thrive. At the start of the 20th century, Japan's ability to leverage technology (particularly in the field of naval engineering), doctrine (e.g., swarm-style tactics—most recently seen off the Horn of Africa by Somali pirates) and politics (challenging the waning Tsar of Russia by seizing Port Arthur in 1904) catapulted them into global prominence. Though their military might was vanquished after

---

[154] This topic is amply covered by both *WIRED* magazine's Danger Room blog (http://blog.wired.com/defense/) and John Robb's Global Guerillas blog (http://globalguerrillas.typepad.com/).

World War II, today Japan is the world's second largest economy in terms of Gross Domestic Product (second only to the United States).

Regardless of whether future conflict is driven by ideology or resources, there is no doubt that the nation-state's monopoly on violence is dwindling. While the aftermath of Westphalia nearly four centuries ago saw the primacy of warfare shift from the Church to the Nation-State, today we are seeing that power diffuse into far more ambiguous social structures.

The emergence of Clausewitz's "Popular Rage" as the primary mechanism of violence will further erode the adequacy of modern force structures and large-scale, platform-dependent conventional militaries. In the U.S. Department of Defense, this foretells a shift in emphasis from the geographically-focused Combatant Commands (as defined in the biannually updated Unified Command Plan) to the U.S. Northern Command[155] and its responsibility to defend, protect and secure the United States and its interests.[156]

This convergence of "military" and "civil" authorities has been a source of debate since the dawn of the republic. Much has been written to constrain the U.S. military's role in law enforcement (e.g., the Posse Comitatus Act of 1878, passed at the end of Reconstruction to prohibit federal military personnel from acting in a law enforcement capacity), yet the missions being asked of our forces today equate to exactly those roles in other nations. In fact, some have even suggested that the expansion of military missions

---

[155] Statement by Hon. Paul McHale, Asst. Sec. of Defense for Homeland Security, before the 108th Congress, Committee on Armed Services, Subcommittee on Terrorism, Unconventional Threats and Capabilities, March 4th 2004.

[156] U.S. Northern Command Mission, http://www.northcom.mil/About/index.html .

into the realm of governance and nation-building is sowing the seeds of our own military *coup d'état*.[157]

Rather than expand the capability set of a specific segment of society, a better approach is to enable *decentralized* response. The U.S. Department of Homeland Security has adopted many "best practices" of the U.S. military and codified them in the National Incident Management System (NIMS) and the Incident Command System (ICS). By standardizing the values of effective management (e.g., unity of effort, span of control and commonality of terms), these systems enhance both local preparedness as well as effective collaboration when incidents exceed local capacity.

Secretary of Defense Robert Gates recently said, "New institutions are needed for the twenty-first century, new organizations with a twenty-first-century mindset."[158] Perhaps ... but we must also dismantle outdated and ineffective institutions and reorient those resources toward more productive ends. Otherwise the bloat of past bureaucracies will undermine any hope for future success.

---

[157] Lt Col C. J. Dunlap, Jr., USAF, "The Origins of the American Military Coup of 2012", National Defense University/National War College (Class of 1992).
[158] *Forging a New Shield,* Project on National Security Reform, November 2008, p. 23.

RECONFIGURING THE NATIONAL SECURITY ARCHITECTURE

SHLOK VAIDYA

The incoming Obama administration is inheriting a critically unstable global system. Errors are being thrown up at every turn as the system fails to gain any governance traction over concurrent threats in the international, domestic, social, environmental, and fiscal domains.

Enormously thick and tall government hierarchies, along with the frameworks that gave rise to them, will cascade and fail, shaking our foundations as they plummet. In many ways, the Obama administration(s) will indeed be centered on "change," though not the stuff of campaign promises. We will watch assumptions—about the capabilities of the military, the infallibility of markets, trust in an elite stratum of the wealthy (supposedly the smartest the world has ever seen)—all collapse as we rush headlong into this future.

A rapidly deteriorating economic environment is, at this point, operating on the fumes of inertia. As the crisis unfolds, even what thin veneer of social mobility is left will be called into question. A regressive slide across the board will accentuate all fault lines within the American social system: race, class, location or religion to list a few. To a significant degree we have been able to bypass, ignore, or overcome these divides over the course of the last decade and a half. Unfortunately, the same flows of globalization and technological progress we once leveraged for opportunity could reverse, threatening our homes, our work, and our communities in the process.

AN OPPORTUNITY

The administration will have to work very quickly to accurately assess and react to these many challenges. Unfortunately, the core levers of government power are generally useless in the modern era. The fiscal system is, at the time of this writing, approaching the monetary policy zero bound. Cities and states are going bankrupt across the country. In short, we will require the development of whole new approaches to governance.

While the new government may work hard towards change with great purpose and tenacity, the current national security architecture is simply not conducive to innovation. This is largely due to the legacy governance systems currently in place that allow much of the insight, capabilities, and ideas generated at the bottom of enormous hierarchies to dissipate.

Over the next four years, while it is possible we may see widespread fracturing of the American nation-state, we are more likely to see the environment emerge for that process to take place under following administrations. By building a national security architecture that allows for rapid reconfiguration when necessary (probably sometime in the next decade), the Obama administration can pioneer next-generation governance. Every action taken by the Obama administration should be focused on equipping this country, its citizens, and its collectives with the ability to cope with an increasingly uncertain future.

CONTROLLED COLLAPSE

The nation-state, our system of governance for the last few hundred years, is failing to match pace with the various technologically empowered elements that seek to undermine its existence. This is trend is easily detectable: Open up your preferred source of news and take note of the many militias operating in states all over the world. In particular, pay attention to the ones that are embraced by the governments in the area, theoretically functioning, as "spontaneous" and "reactive" to a terrorist-spawned impetus. Each is a myth built to perpetuate the façade of a state. The mere existence of such militias undermines the nation-state.

This same dynamic could easily take hold at home. We are already seeing it emerge to some degree as cities institute foreclosure moratoriums in response to bank orders to remove families from their homes. The question is how to control this transfer of power and prevent chaos—that which is detrimental to prosperity and ultimately a more secure future.

THE NATIONAL SECURITY ARCHITECTURE

Any strategy to mitigate the threat of chaos will have to center on building a new national security architecture that is, instead of being grounded in wars of old, able to scale with a focus on a rapidly unfolding unknown future. This will be largely local, and thus have to be done cheaply. With the correct design philosophy, it will be a model that can be easily adapted to different communities with different requirements.

Our current national security system (the national-level organizations, comprised of the Department of Homeland Security, the Department of Defense, the entire Intelligence Community, the FBI) was compiled over time to mitigate and approach individual security threats. Rather than utilizing any discernible design philosophy, its architects simply added layers of complexity, in the form of organizations and bureaucracy layers, in an ad-hoc fashion. For example, the number of executive titles in government has increased some 400% since 1960, in no small part due to the Global War on Terror. The latest, and largest iteration of this strategy is the Department of Homeland Security. Over that same time span we have seen a marked decline in the quality of service provided (notably marked by failing on 9/11, the run-up to the war in Iraq, the wars in Iraq and Afghanistan, the response to Hurricane Katrina).

This lack of performance is largely due to a decision on the part of policymakers to forego competition, which increases the quality of service and decreases overhead costs. Instead, Washington insiders guaranteed a massive budget for the national security superstructure that is in no way, as demonstrated above, tethered to reality or success. This allowed the structure to ossify, rendering it unable to retain any level of flexibility—a major short falling when we face an enemy that has repeatedly demonstrated an ability to outmaneuver and outthink us.

PLATFORM THINKING

Blazing-fast communication, highly distributed modern computing power, and ever cheaper data storage allows hierarchies to implode, individuals to act on a global level, and organizations to operate faster, leaner, and more effectively. Unfortunately, this potential has not been harnessed by the ossifying national security architecture. In fact, the inability to successfully harness information management technology has accelerated the ossification process. Remedying this is one major step forward. But this idea goes much deeper than technology, which does not amount to much more than an enabling mechanism.

The lessons of successful technology platforms could revolutionize the nature of governance in the United States. What follows is some short thinking that should help readers consider how best to adapt the structures around them to better sustain and mitigate security shocks.

OVERVIEW

The primary purpose of a security platform is to stockpile and easily make available information to various players (nodes), situation specific task forces (planks), and long-term enablers (stacks). Each relies on the others to comprise an effective system, but the taxonomy proves useful in understanding the structure.

THE NODES

All governance is local. All security crises are local as well. This is often lost in a world that is so tightly interconnected that YouTube and Twitter are able to magnify a security event along peer-to-peer lines. The effects of terrorism are trans- and international in nature, but the acts themselves are hard bounded to the target in question. Unfortunately, our national and international coping mechanisms, rapid response forces, and long term approaches have failed to understand this dynamic.

Rather than the players in the national security architecture of old, such as the CIA, NSA, FBI, or even Navy, Army, Marines and Air Force, our real defense actors are police officers, firemen, medical first responders, private security forces, the private sector, the media, and ourselves. In short, anyone who can gain, process, or transmit knowledge is a "node" on the security network.

THE PLANKS

In response to systemic shocks, such as a bank robbery (hyperlocal), the crashing of a core infrastructure system (regional), or biological warfare attack (national) modular nodes connect, communicate, and act in concert with one another. When these nodes combine with one another, the combination is a "plank" of shock-specific services at each progressively larger area of governance. Allowing these planks to be modular equates to greater efficiency and lower overhead while freeing up other assets to prepare for other (potential) shocks.

We have seen planks develop in response to shocks over the past decade. The fires in Southern California catalyzed, armies of nodes (planks) to build web applications to better inform the public and provide actionable data for those still in the region. The same type of response was observed in response to the late November attacks in Mumbai, the 2004 Tsunami, and Hurricane Katrina.

THE STACKS

While the first two components of a platform are already live, already being independently built and utilized by millions of citizens, the final component will require some work on the part of the Obama administration. These nodes and planks require capabilities in order to better connect to one another. They are incredibly innovative and often operate on shoestring budgets, but some investments are simply too costly, can't be done on the fly, or require significant fulltime focus that most planks won't be able to provide. "Stacks" are core platform services provided by the U.S. government to better enable the nodes distributed throughout the country. This is largely based on the government's superior collective buying power.

Some possible stacks, essentially very, very lean versions of current agencies include:

- Communications platform. To monitor and ensure the edges along critical communications grids.

- Acquisitions platform. To enable the buying and selling of weapons and other equipment both among the planks as well as for them (group buys).

- Intelligence platform. To build analytical products designed for maximum consumption (rather than the status quo of varying levels of classification). This will require a generational shift, as well as a massive cultural one.

- Military platform. To mostly provide specialized training, though also coordinate the response to larger threats.

- Central administrative platform. A highly leveraged, highly paid small private sector team to coordinate the various stacks and ensure the platform is running correctly.

This will be the most revolutionary component of a new national security architecture and will center on exploding the status quo, and allowing the nodes to pick up the pieces and do what they will. If leveraged, President Obama will find them to be smart, highly motivated, and effective. Nodes and planks are already at play in domains as varied as education, energy, and social structure.

CONCLUSION

The likelihood of seeing this new flexible, agile and valuable structure emerge as part of a concentrated government program is very, very slim. This security system configuration will be troublesome, if not offensive, to most of the old guard. The military plays a small role if it plays one at all. If change is successful, wreckages of massive hierarchies that concentrate wealth, power, and drive a military-industrial complex would litter the future landscape. However, the alternative is that it would rise organically, though only after the global situation, and America's in particular, deteriorated significantly more than it already has, and also most likely after President Obama has already left office.

In most ways, the next four to eight years will be revolutionary, transitory, a time of fast-paced change, creative and destructive chaos. If President Obama wants to sustain long-term change, the thinking provided here could prove useful should he find it necessary to implement deep structural changes that will allow the powerhouse of innovation that is the American people to take control of their destinies in very uncertain times. It is time to fortify and lay the groundwork for our coping mechanisms.

A GRAND STRATEGY FOR A NETWORKED CIVILIZATION

MARK SAFRANSKI

In 330 AD, Constantine the Great, having reunified the Roman Empire and reorganized the Christian Church, consecrated his "New Rome" at the site of old Byzantium. Called Constantinople, the city would reign over an Eastern empire for a thousand years, dying at the hands of the Ottoman Turks only a scant four decades before Columbus discovered the New World. A thousand years before Constantine stood on the shores of the Bosporus, the legendary lawgiver Lycurgus gave the Spartans a constitution that would endure for seven centuries. By contrast, Charles V of Spain squandered an unparalleled strategic opportunity to put a Spanish Hapsburg stamp on European civilization by dissipating his energies on endless small wars of religion and dividing his inheritance. Spain's undisputed superpower glory was but brief.

Whether rulers sink their plans into the bedrock of history or build castles of sand depends heavily on mastering the art of the long view, of the historian peering into the future. It takes a careful eye to correctly discern the events of the day but looking ahead decades or centuries is the most difficult prospect of all. The National Intelligence Council periodically convenes experts, futurists and intel analysts to bravely map out only the next seventeen years.[159] Our science fiction writers can see farther than our statesmen because politicians and bureaucrats are concerned with the bark on a tree rather than the health of the forest. At pivotal points in history, a society needs leaders with the perspective of eagles. 21st century America appears to be at such a turning point but we find eagles to be in short supply. What

---

[159] "Global Trends 2025:A Transformed World".
http://www.dni.gov/nic/NIC_2025_project.html

Washington has in excess are woodpeckers—whole flocks of them—and they generate more noise than they do vision.

Some may object here that the ancients "had it easy." The pace of life moved more slowly in preindustrial ages which gave rulers time to ponder before they acted. This excuse is nonsensical. It is not a question of "speed" alone but of life's complexity relative to the velocity at which information could travel and the ability of the ruler and his servants to distill meaning from the complexity in the information they received. Xerxes' Persian satraps and the Mongols of Genghis Khan administered immense geographic domains with only the aid of primitive warning beacons and men on horseback. The Incas did it with men on foot. Is the level of complexity America faces today insurmountably greater than the chaos and civil war that Constantine inherited from the failure of Diocletian's imperial reforms?

The difference between leaders today and those in the past—not only past centuries but as recently as the Cold War—is a certain loss of perspective as to longitudinal scale and societal fundamentals. American politicians think primarily in terms of the present, mentally cycling with the nightly news or the upcoming elections, which give more weight to superficial, tactical, objectives than they deserve and waste time, resources and opportunities. Not only has the political will to make long term, strategic investments in the national interest faded, it is questionable as to the degree to which they are even considered. The current economic crisis requires action, naturally, but if the incoming Obama administration wishes to make their mark on history, they should give at least as much thought to 2100 as they do to 2010.

How does one look so far ahead? The place to begin is with realism about what variables matter over a yawning stretch of time and humility about our ability to influence them. Some of the changes that will occur during the course of the 21st century will be of a technological nature and are therefore, very hard to predict given the "leap capacity" inherent to scientific discovery. Nevertheless, more stable elements crucial to facilitating national power and prosperity exist that are profoundly relevant in making probabilistic, grand strategic, assessments. We also have historical examples of statesmen and scholars who have tried to do exactly that with visions that were a synthesis of the predictive as well as the prescriptive and were, on balance, remarkable in their analytical clarity.

The earliest political philosophers among the Greeks, Romans, Chinese and Arabs sifted society for meta-patterns of behavior in an effort to explain the art of politics and especially, the phenomena of revolutions. Their identification of *cyclical change* in the nature of government was frequently ascribed to either the moral decay of the ruler (Confucius, Plato) or of the ruled (Polybius, Ibn Khaldun). This societal degeneration stemmed from the corruption of power leading to avarice and tyranny and from violating the primal rules (Cicero, Mencius) that underpinned their "mandate of heaven" or "legitimacy." To forfeit the mandate was to invite violent revolution.

The solutions offered by these philosophers to delay the moral and political decay of the state essentially fell into camps: enshrining a dictatorship of virtue that commanded sufficient power to regiment society (Plato, Han Fei-tzu) or creating a "mixed form of government" that would naturally check strengths and balance weaknesses (Aristotle, Polybius). History has vindicated the second approach. The negative examples of the bloody record of the French Revolution through the murderous totalitarian dictatorships of the 20th century attest to the ruinous costs of perfecting society by force. Imperfect as we are, "moral legitimacy" as defined by the people a government seeks to rule or influence, remains a bedrock strategic variable.

Less persuasive than the ancient philosophers, but a group whose arguments are not entirely without merit, are the historians, geopolitical and naval strategists of the 19th and 20th centuries who were deeply concerned with the consequences of place and space on national power or national "character". Friedrich Ratzel, Sir Halford Mackinder, Rudolf Kjellen, Frederick Jackson Turner, Alfred T. Mahan and Sir Julian Corbett articulated in different ways the political and military implications that the comparative advantages of territory or distance conveyed in international conflict. Some of their arguments have been proven wrong or are brazenly racialist and unscientific, almost mystical in their assumptions, particularly those of the German *Geopolitik* school.It is difficult however, to disregard geographic considerations in calculating future possibilities. Even if the cultural influence of geography on national psyches should be taken in stride, cultural mores and attitudes have a deep impact on national development.

The international system is biased against casual changes in the borders of states and political borders represent relatively stable demarcations of resources and a platform for economic and political activity. Distance creates costs in terms of time and money and it is illogical to expect Singapore or the Netherlands would develop national strategies and economic flows that resemble those of Russia or Brazil. While location isn't everything, it still matters.

Closer to our own time, and a model for the task at hand, is strategic futurism from an economic determinist perspective, epitomized by Brooks Adams. Descendent of two presidents, Brooks Adams was a historian and an intellectual powerhouse who served as part of Theodore Roosevelt's circle of advisers, alongside his brother, Henry Adams, Frederick Jackson Turner, John Hay, Henry Cabot Lodge, Alfred T. Mahan and Elihu Root. It was Brooks Adams who first forecast the coming of the Great War as early as 1898 and faulted an imperial and protectionist global trade regime for causing it. Adams warned contemporaries of a fading British

Empire, the impending strategic danger of German hegemony, America as a garrison-state and still decades- distant challenges to America by Russia and China. Such prescience is rare.

A proponent of cyclical theories of historical change, Adams rooted his analysis in the momentum of global forces of the market (which dismayed him) and national economic potential. Overshadowed by the literary talent of his famous brother Henry, Brooks wrote the deeper and more reflective books. His *The Law of Civilization and Decay, America's Economic Supremacy* and *Theory of Social Revolution* all belong on the shelf of any serious futurist or strategist. Adams was the forerunner of later Anglo-American figures who grasped the connection between the state of the global economic system and the prospects for American power and prosperity. A tradition continued by John Maynard Keynes, Bernard Baruch, Cordell Hull, Winston Churchill, Henry Stimson, Franklin Roosevelt, Harry Truman, George Kennan, Dean Acheson, George Marshall, John Foster Dulles, Paul Nitze and others who understood, despite their partisan and policy differences, the interdependent and interrelated nature of economic, political and military power.

Moral legitimacy of the state, the nature of the homeland it governs and the political economy that satisfies the needs of the people are the fundamentals of strategic calculation; the longer the time frame to be considered, the more that getting the fundamentals right matters. Exotic methodological tools, supercomputers and quantitative analysis all have their place—they illuminate the nuances of both the real as well as the possible. They are the hammer and chisel of the futurist sculptor while the fundamentals are the block of marble

Nor does this mean that transient concerns, discoveries, small wars and short events trends count for nothing—they most certainly do and can have large, even epochal, implications. "Black

Swan" events that perturb the whole system have special significance and alter historical trajectories[160]; however, Black Swans are by definition unforeseen and all these great and small factors occur and act in the context of the variables that compose the strategic baseline and it is that baseline that we must try to shape for the 22nd century and beyond.

What should be done so that America greets the year 2100 as a global power with security and influence abroad and prosperity and peace at home ?

DEMOGRAPHICS

A reality that eludes most Americans, many of whom lived through the "population bomb" and "Club of Rome" 1970's is the extent to which the coming decades will see the rapid aging of our friends and foes alike. By 2040 the furious cauldron of today's Mideast with its "youth bulge" will be a middle-aged region where "bulge" would refer to the 42 inch waistlines of the people. Countries like Russia and Germany will literally be dying off, as will Southern Africa, which is already in negative population growth due to AIDS. Japan and China will be "Asian Floridas" with exploding senior populations. Grand strategist Thomas P.M. Barnett writes of this radical demographic shift in *Great Powers: America and the World After Bush*:

> "... By pursuing the one-child policy and basically wiping a slice of their population off of the books...China set in motion a demographic wave that currently places them in a sweet spot that they must continue exploiting for all it's worth.... By 2030, China will have an elderly population roughly the size of the United States, meaning, in my opinion, that China is

---

[160] Taleb, Nicholas Nassim. 2007. *The Black Swan: The Impact of the Highly Improbable*. (New York. Random House: 2007). Xvii-xxviii, 44-50, 272-273

likely to pass us in age before ever possibly passing us in overall economic size.[161]

Economic dynamism is a result of many variables but one of them is a younger median age population. Like most of the developed world, the United States is aging but unlike most of the world, the United States historically can tolerate and reap the economic benefits of far higher levels of immigration than can China, Germany or Japan. Our identity is ideological, rooted in the Constitution and the Declaration of Independence rather than a protean racial, tribal, or religious attachment to "blood and soil."

Therefore, instead of leaving immigration policy hostage to the desire of Big Business for an exploitable, cheap, labor force and the PC demands of established ethnic lobbies, the U.S. should treat immigration as a strategic tool of national economic growth. We should aim to drive our median age *downward* to the late 20's by favoring younger immigrants, even at the cost of considerably higher net population growth than current projections. Secondly, the United States should radically diversify the immigrant pool to new geographic regions.

This will mean junking LBJ era immigration law and "family reunification" policies while retaining robustly high overall rates of immigration but imposing a *drastic* reduction in immigration rates (legal and illegal) from Mexico while initiating a *dramatic* increase for underrepresented regions like Central and Eastern Asia, Eastern Europe, South America and Africa. The United States will benefit from a larger, more linguistically multicultural and globally connected population of prime working age, relative to retirees. The political fight to change immigration policy will be as bitter as only the overthrowing of narrow and entrenched special interests

---

[161] Barnnett, Thomas P.M. *Great Powers:America and the World After Bush.* (New York. G.P. Putnam & Sons, 2009.). P.185-186.

can be but the dividends of such a change will be manifold and long term. An America of 650 million in 2100 will be cause for celebration.

MORAL LEGITIMACY

Improving what military strategist Colonel John Boyd would have called America's "fitness" as a society is imperative not only to thrive in the 22nd century as a great power but perhaps just to survive to reach it as well. We must change our ways or lose the game.

Technological trend lines are running heavily against the nation-state if they continue operating in the traditional manner of the last 400 years. The Westphalian society of states have relied upon the certitude of their ability to bring massive force to bear to *punish* enemies in order to expand their authority at home and abroad. This paradigm is already passing into history, a process that historian Martin van Creveld argues is the inevitable "decline of the state."[162] A less dystopian analysis would be to say that liberal, capitalist, nation-states are becoming the victims of their own extraordinary success. Having *intentionally* generated enormous wealth and connectivity in the form of globalization, spawned IGOs, NGOs and facilitated the rise of non-state actors, nation-states must now evolve to adapt to the environment created by fifty years of postwar Western grand strategy.

Modern states of advanced countries now find themselves with vast authority over a wide spectrum of activity beyond their capacity to give sufficient bureaucratic attention, except upon a crisis management basis. Nor are the rigid bureaucracies, most of which were created decades ago for a mass-production society, knowledgeable or nimble enough to cope with accelerating rates of

---

[162] Creveld, Martin van. *The Rise and Decline of the State* at 336-421. (New York:. Cambridge University Press, 1999).

technological innovation or complexity. The breakdown in the "orientation" phase of the state's OODA Loop coincides with the increasing capability of groups and individuals to not only evade or resist the claims of governments or if sufficiently aggrieved, to hit back with soft or hard power options. It is not that states are now powerless or are obsolete but the emergence of players with countervailing leverage have exposed the limits of nation-state power.

Nation-states in the 21ˢᵗ century will face a complex international ecosystem of players rather than just the society of states envisioned by traditional *realpolitik*. If the predictions offered by serious thinkers such as Ray Kurzweil, Fred Ikle or John Robb prove true, then technological breakthroughs will ensure the emergence of "superempowered individuals"[163] on a sizable scale in the near future. At that moment, the reliance of the State on its' punitive powers as a weapon of first resort comes to an end. Superempowered individuals, separatist groups, insurgents and an "opting-out" citizenry will nibble recalcitrant and unpopular states to death, hollowing them out and transferring their allegiance elsewhere.

While successful states will retain punitive powers, their primary focus will become *attracting* followers and clients in whom they can generate intense or at least dependable, loyalty and leverage as a networked system to pursue national interests. This represents a shift from worldview of enforcement to one of empowerment, coordination and collaboration. States will be forced to narrow their scope of activity from trying to supervise everything to flexibly providing or facilitating core services, platforms, rule-sets and opportunities—critical public goods—that the private sector or social groups cannot easily replicate or replace. Outside of a vital

---

[163] Safranski, Mark. Oct. 8 2006. "The Super Empowered individual". http://zenpundit.blogspot.com/2006/10/super-empowered-individual-man-is.html

core of activity, the state becomes an arbiter among the lesser, interdependent, quasi-autonomous, powers to which it is connected.

Philip Bobbitt has used the term "market-state" as a descriptor [164] but the function of a 21st century state in this capacity is going to be cognitive or cultural as well as material, promoting authentic values which citizens and prospective immigrants or clients can identify, internalize and be motivated to defend. The "value chains" of concepts (to borrow a term from Michael Wilson)[165] are the building blocks of what John Boyd called "a noble philosophy" that permits a social contract to be a powerful tool of "vitality and growth," attracting admiration and commanding allegiance.[166] Demonstration of fidelity to expressed values in policy and actions is also the yardstick for citizens measuring the moral legitimacy of the state's performance

The United States will have both an easy and a difficult time making a transition to a world where even the great power nation-states are simply at the top of a complex and dynamically shifting food chain rather than each state existing as a virtual universe unto themselves. Easy, because the ideological narrative of "the American dream" and a decentralized structure of Federalism and limited government of shared powers is a microcosm of such a world; difficult, because standing at the apex of the old Westphalian state system, the U.S. has much to lose with its demise. The temptation to resist erosion of sovereign authority at each instance, rather than to make strategic choices over what

---

[164] Bobbitt, Philip. *The Shield of Achilles* at 228-242. (New York, NY. Anchor Books, 2002)

[165] Wilson, Michael. 2001. " The Social Contract, Value Chain and dependency Infrastructures". http://www.metatempo.com/SocialContract.PDF

[166] Boyd, John. "Patterns of Conflict". 1981. http://www.chetrichards.com/modern_business_strategy/boyd/patterns/insight_and_elaboration.ht

areas of governance to defend, will be very great. However, given its great reserves of wealth and power as the preeminent state in the world, the U.S. could alternatively invest its resources early in determining the rule-sets regarding what activities or areas states genuinely need to control in order to remain viable and effective authorities vs. those areas that can be safely ceded or negotiated before the stakeholders are strong enough to wrest control from the state on their own terms.

GEOGRAPHY AS DESTINY

Aside from potentially revolutionary developments in technology, the wild card in determining America's position in 2100 ad will be changes in international borders. Despite the strong post-WWII bias in international law against changing national boundaries, especially through military conquest, the late 20th and early 21st century has been a period of dramatic aggregation, expansion and discorporation of multinational states. There is no evidence to believe that this historical trend toward instability has crested, and current circumstances indicate that the odds of geopolitical upheaval in coming decades are excellent.

The collapse of the Soviet Union bequeathed Stalin's ethnographic legacy to its successor states, including Russia: irrational borders that replicate the multi-ethnic, "molten pot" of chauvinistic majority and uneasy, transnational minorities of the old USSR. Russia houses at least 100 different ethnic groups, including Chechens and Tatars who seek greater autonomy while almost every "near abroad" state has a politically sensitive, "tripwire," Russian minority or pro-Russian "little brother" ethnic group like Georgia's Ossetians and Abkhazians. China's leadership fears any sustained social unrest or Taiwanese independence could trigger a new round of the centrifugal disintegration that marks China's long history while rising India is home to two thousand ethnic groups and eight serious insurgencies active in at least half of India's states. Africa's largest and most populous states—Nigeria,

Congo, Sudan—are failed or failing states, as is much of the sub-Saharan core of central Africa that has seen 3 million dead from a decade of ethnic warfare and an AIDS pandemic.

At the other end of the spectrum, the EU and to a lesser degree, NAFTA, point the way toward peaceful nation-state aggregation into a supranational entity for mutual economic benefit and geopolitical leverage. Economic unions can predate durable political unions or at least encourage enduring strategic partnerships. The OAU, Arab League, OAS and the UN are feckless because they provide few economic incentives in their existence that would lead their memberships to cooperate constructively or take unified action. The contours of "natural" market exchange provide borders that are often more real and significant than imaginary lines on a map.

The combination of global instability and economic connectivity gives the United States the greatest opportunity for shaping the future, leveraging 4GW centripetal forces here and centrifugal economic connectivity there, to yield nonzero sum gains for itself and the global system as a whole. As the U.S. should be content to grow its population to gain economic advantages over the course of the 21st century, it should also aggressively but peacefully grow its "space" territorially, as suggested by Thomas Barnett, or economically through market-security IGO or new entities yet to be devised.[167] Supranational market organizations—say, hypothetically a "Pacific Rim Community" stretching from India to Chile and then to Australia—weave overarching connectivity and generate rule-sets that strengthen the system and build environments that can "catch" fragmenting or failing states.

---

[167] Barnett, Thomas P.M. " The Next Five States". Esquire. September 19, 2007. http://www.esquire.com/features/esquire-100/fivestates1007

The beauty of the process is that economic connectivity can build structures that cut across culture-centric identity patterns as well as reinforce them, permitting real, long-term, strategic choices. The 19th century German *Zollervein* proposal presaged German unification, setting off a historical trajectory that was resolved when the Schumann Plan engineered a Franco-German unity over coal, leading directly to the birth of the EU at the end of 20th. The global communities we build to be adjunctive to our nation may in time be virtual and informational rather than physical, or perhaps in time even extra-planetary. Great centers of cultural dynamism in history expand and fuse with other domains to create something new; Alexander ushered in not a Greek Empire but a Hellenistic Age that spanned from the Ptolemaic Nile to the Greco-Buddhist kingdoms on the banks of the Syr Darya. The conceptual target for American statesmen who look far ahead should not be the United States, the mere nation-state or the superpower but building the United States as a networked civilization.

To set a good foundation is to build for the Ages.

www.ingramcontent.com/pod-product-compliance
Lightning Source LLC
Chambersburg PA
CBHW080330270326
41927CB00014B/3152